FLATBUSH

THE HEART OF BROOKLYN

Ocean and Newkirk Avenues before 1920. The Ditmas Park Historic District houses, designed by architect George Pilliser for George Van Ness and Thomas Brush, 1000 and 1010 Ocean Avenue respectively, were singled out by the New York City Landmarks Preservation Commission as excellent examples of an "innovative application of the Colonial Revival style."

Front Cover: *Flatbush Avenue* c. *1950. (Courtesy Marsh Davis and Ron Schweiger.)*

THE MAKING OF AMERICA

FLATBUSH

THE HEART OF BROOKLYN

NEDDA C. ALLBRAY

ARCADIA PUBLISHING

ISBN 978-0-7385-2453-5

Published by Arcadia Publishing
Charleston, South Carolina

Printed in the United States of America

Library of Congress Catalog Card Number: 2003111121

For all general information contact Arcadia Publishing at:
Telephone 843-853-2070
Fax 843-853-0044
E-Mail sales@arcadiapublishing.com
For customer service and orders:
Toll-Free 1-888-313-2665

Visit us on the Internet at www.arcadiapublishing.com

CONTENTS

ACKNOWLEDGMENTS

I would like to thank Prospect Park South Association, the Ditmas Park Association, the Flatbush Development Corporation, the New York State Archives, the Historic District Council of New York, Mary Kay Gallagher of Mary Kay Gallagher Real Estate, and Brooklyn Historian Ron Schweiger for their contributions. And most of all a special thank you to my husband, Igou M. Allbray, who supported the project and when needed also became chief—although often unacknowledged—photographer.

PROLOGUE

Today Flatbush, Brooklyn, is a vibrant urban community. Only the First Reformed Dutch Church—its white steeple soaring skyward, its quiet churchyard a place of tranquility amidst the commotion of city life—stands as a public reminder of a pastoral past. This is the story of the Dutch town of Flatbush, one of the oldest European settlements in America, as it evolved from a village of successful farmers to a suburb for New York City's prosperous middle class, and finally into a quintessential urban community that is a microcosm of New York City's diversity.

A Golden Age: 1609–1630

In 1609 Henry Hudson, an English sea captain flying the Dutch flag, sailed into New York harbor and continued up the great river that today bears his name. Hudson, like all European explorers at the time, was seeking a faster trade route to the riches of the Far East. What he found was a land of virgin forests of white and black oak, pine, and hemlock that were rich in animals such as muskrat, beaver, and fox whose furs were in high demand on the European markets. Based on his voyage the Dutch laid claim to the lands from the Delaware River north, along both sides of the Hudson, to Fort Orange (Albany) as New Netherlands, a claim that put them into conflict with the English who had already established settlements in the surrounding areas.

Seventeenth-century Holland was enjoying a golden age, a period of peace and great prosperity. Unlike the English, who were empire builders and controlled their lands politically through the crown, the Dutch were merchants who saw New Netherlands as a commercial enterprise. In order to exploit the riches of the new lands fully, a merchant syndicate, the Dutch West India Company (DWI), modeled after the successful Dutch East India Company, was organized in 1621. It was given control of New Netherlands with exclusive rights to the lucrative fur trade.

Initially Dutch colonization did not seem imperative. However, quickly, the company directors and the Dutch government realized that trappers and traders in the sparsely populated land were a too small and too unstable population to sustain their claims. It was necessary to create permanent settlements, but this was difficult for the Dutch. In contrast to England, where dissident groups were willing to leave their homeland and face hardship in order to form their own communities, the Dutch were reluctant to forsake the comforts and freedoms of Holland, which at the time was the most liberal and tolerant country in Europe. In order to entice people to the dangerous and unsettled land, in 1639 the Dutch government stepped in and in addition to offering farmers and their families free passage and the opportunity to acquire as much land as they could clear and farm, the government removed the DWI's monopoly over the fur trade. The opportunity for land and the potential for farming attracted some Dutch, who were joined by Walloons from Belgium, Huguenots from France, Germans, and Scandinavians. Later, beginning in 1654, Jews and in 1657 Quakers were permitted entry. Although Governor General Peter Stuyvesant protested the Jews, the DWI, in which many of Holland's Jewish merchants had invested, overrode his opposition and, in the interest of continued immigration, insisted on maintaining a policy of tolerance. This did not mean that the Jews were fully accepted, however. In 1655 the Burgher Council of New Amsterdam excluded all Jews from serving in the militia and then taxed each Jewish male between the ages of sixteen and sixty an amount of 65 stivers (approximately $1.30) per month in lieu of military service. On the other hand, although the Jews and other religious minorities were not allowed to build houses of worship, they were permitted to practice their religion in private. Thus, perhaps in spite of themselves, New Amsterdam and its sister Dutch settlements from their beginnings showed far greater tolerance for diversity than their English counterparts. This diversity continued to distinguish Dutch settlements—and the lands that they settled—even after the English conquered them in 1664.

The first Dutch colony was established in 1624 at Fort Orange (Albany) and consisted of thirty Dutch and Belgium Walloon families. The settlement failed. Without the political or spiritual motivation that drove many of the English colonists, most of the settlers were discouraged by the harshness of their lives and returned to Europe after completing their contract year. Those who did stay, for reasons of safety and consolidation, were moved back to New Amsterdam in 1626. In the same year the Dutch West India Company, in an attempt to turn what appeared to be a failing venture into a profitable one, began importing slaves with the hope that the promise of free labor would serve as a further inducement for colonists to stay.

Settlement on Western Long Island: 1630–1664

Although there had been settlement in the area earlier, the recorded land history of the towns that became Flatbush and Flatlands begins in 1635. A deed from that year between the Canarsee Indians and Jacobus van Corlear shows that a tract of land, which became known as Corlear flats, was purchased. Shortly thereafter, in 1636, the Canarsees deeded nearby tracts of land to Andries Hedden and to Wolphert Gerritsen van Couwenhoven (Kouenhoven) for the area known as Little Flats and to Governor General Wouter Van Twiller for land that became known as Twiller's Flats. Another land purchase in the area was made at the same time by Hans Hansen Bergen, who had immigrated to Holland from Norway and from there to New Netherlands. As the town of Flatbush grew, the portion of the woodlands around it that included Corlear Flats and Twiller's Flats were held common by the residents of the town until they were sold at the end of the eighteenth century in order to help pay for the construction of the Erasmus Academy, one of the first secular high schools in New York.

The DWI required that land be purchased from native peoples, who in Brooklyn were the Canarsee Indians. Since exclusive land ownership was not part of their culture, however, the Canarsees were angered to learn that under European law the exchanges meant the newcomers were given permanent possession of their lands. In 1670 Eskemoppas, the Sachem (chief) of the Rockaways and his two brothers took advantage of this stricture and asserted ownership of the lands. They claimed that they, not the Canarsees, owned Flatbush, for which they demanded payment. The Dutch farmers claimed they had already paid for the land, but to avoid hostility a second payment was made. (See box on page 65.) That incident notwithstanding, the two groups lived in the area without serious clashes, although the settlers early on were ordered to build protective fortifications as a precaution.

One of the earliest Dutch settlements on Long Island was Nieuw Amersfoort (Flatlands). The absence of trees and the flat landscape of the place reminded the settlers from the lowlands of the homes they had left behind. But this land had none of the amenities of their home country. Farming was hard, made tougher at first because the work had to be done without farm animals. The settlers found too that the land was not as rich and productive as they had hoped it would be. Almost immediately some of them left in search of better land. They followed an established Indian trail (today's Flatbush Avenue) north or inland. These colonists settled in a forested area they called by two names: Midwout (middle wood, also spelled as Midwoud and Medwoud), or Vlachtebos (wooded plain). Until the name was finally anglicized as Flatbush, Vlachtebos too had alternative spellings, including Flackebos, Vlacke Bos, and Vlactebos. Various documents including wills and deeds from as early as the seventeenth century indicate that Midwout and Vlachtebos were used interchangeably.

There are also several reasons given for the names. Teunis G. Bergen, a scion of one of the earliest and most prominent families, whose papers included a thorough genealogy of Flatbush, claimed that Medwoud was named for villages in North Holland. Others, according to Gertrude Lefferts Vanderbilt, author of *A Social History of Flatbush* (1882), "give the name a different derivation, and say that it does not come from 'woud,' a forest, but from 'woon' or 'woonen,' to dwell, having reference to the people who lived in the middle district." The most widely accepted reason for both Midwout and Vlachtebos, however, seems to be geography. The name of Flatbush, it was said, distinguished the area from the barren Flatlands to its south, and the name Midwout was to locate it between Flatlands to its south and Brooklyn (Breueklen) to its north.

The terminal moraine, a steep ridge formed by the Wisconsin glacier of the last ice age, separated Flatbush and Brooklyn. This ridge, which would be of major importance in the Battle of Brooklyn during the American Revolution, made travel between the towns difficult. Nevertheless, the two towns fought over their exact boundary. At the Court of Sessions held at Gravesend on December 18, 1678, after the English had gained control of New Netherlands, Jacques Cortelyou and Richard Stillwell were appointed, with the consent of the towns, to set the boundaries. Five years later on June 21, 1683, they reported back to the court that the border had been marked. One of the prominent markers was a large white oak tree, thereafter known as the Dongan

Oak, named for the English Governor Thomas Dongan who had helped settle the dispute. The tree stood below the ridge on its south slope in what is now Prospect Park. It was later felled as part of the American defense of Flatbush Pass during the Battle of Brooklyn, the first and largest engagement of the American Revolution after the Declaration of Independence was signed.

Although hardly noticeable today, the ridge had an important effect on the development of the towns. Following the Revolution, the town of Brooklyn, on the north side of the ridge facing onto the harbor opposite Manhattan, experienced a rapid increase in population. By the start of the Civil War in 1861 it had become the third largest city in America, growing from a population of 1,603 in 1790 to 96,838 in 1850. Ten years later, after annexing the towns of Bushwick and Williamsburg, its population reached 266,661. On the other hand, the four towns on the south side of the ridge (Flatbush, Flatlands, New Utrecht, and the English town of Gravesend) maintained their character as small sparsely populated farming villages until the last decades of the nineteenth century. For example, in 1790 the population of Flatbush, the largest of the towns, was 941. By 1850 it had grown to 3,177, and ten years later its population had only grown by 294 more people to 3,471. That population figure is deceiving, however, since in 1852 the town of New Lots split from Flatbush and in the 1860 census it reported a population of 3,271.

In the last decades of the nineteenth century, the pressures of an exploding population caved to the pressures of urbanization. These pressures were fueled by immigration from southern and eastern Europe combined with technological advances, including the completion of the three bridges spanning the East River (the Brooklyn Bridge in 1883, the Williamsburg Bridge in 1903, and the Manhattan Bridge in 1909) and improvements in road and rail transportation to the "rural" towns, especially Flatbush. Among the most important changes were the opening of Prospect Park in 1868, the beginning of train service on the Coney Island Railroad (now the Q train of the Brighton Beach Subway line, which began ten years later in 1878), and the introduction of the electric trolley car in 1890. In Flatbush, farms that had been held by generations of the same family were subdivided and sold to developers for housing.

Today, what once was the town of Midwout or Vlachtebos is divided into three very distinct sections: Flatbush, Midwood, and East Flatbush. Flatbush, the subject of this book, once incorporated the areas known as Midwood and East Flatbush. Although as early as the late seventeenth century, an area east of the old town of Flatbush was regularly called Ostwout (east woods). Ostwout later became New Lots, which broke away from Flatbush and became a separate town in 1852. Today Flatbush is bounded on the north by the Parade Grounds, Prospect Park, and Empire Boulevard; on the east by Rogers Avenue, which separates it from East Flatbush; on the south by an east-west cut of the Long Island Railroad (located between Avenues H and I), which divides it from Midwood; and on the west by Coney Island Avenue, a major north-south thoroughfare that extends from Prospect Park on the north to the edge of the Atlantic Ocean at Brighton Beach on the south.

Chapter One

FLATBUSH BEFORE THE AMERICAN REVOLUTION

"It was Brooklyn's destiny to help save New Netherlands by becoming a prosaic farm community; a region of plain boers [farmers] and bouweries [farms]."
—Ralph Foster Weld, *Brooklyn is America*

Although the first European settlers arrived in Flatbush as early as the 1620s, the first known land purchase was not made until 1635, and the area was not officially recognized as a town until 1652 when Governor General Peter (Petrus) Stuyvesant granted it a formal charter or land patent. Flatbush was the fourth of what eventually would be six independent towns—five Dutch and one English—on western Long Island. Flatlands (Nieuw Amersfoort) received the first land patent in 1636. The second town, Gravesend, was granted a charter in 1645. It was settled by the English followers of Lady Deborah Moody, the first woman to receive a land patent in the new world. As Anabaptists, Lady Moody's group had been driven out of New England. In the more liberal and diverse New Netherlands they found a place where they could practice their religion freely. The third town, Brooklyn (Breukelen), received its charter in 1646. In 1652 Flatbush (Midwout or Vlachtebos) was next, followed by New Utrecht in 1657, and Bushwick (Bosyck) in 1660.

Unlike the English towns, including Gravesend, which were planned around town squares for reasons of safety, Flatbush was organized linearly. The houses, like all Dutch farmhouses, were built facing south along the east and west sides of what was then a narrow winding Indian trail and is now Flatbush Avenue, the only street that completely traverses Brooklyn stretching from the Manhattan Bridge on the north to the Marine Parkway Bridge to the Rockaways on the south. The houses were low, rarely more than one and a half stories tall, and broad—the southern exposure along their long wall maximized daylight. The farms (bouweries) were laid out behind the houses as forty-eight narrow oblong lots, approximately twenty-seven Dutch rods wide by 600 Dutch rods long. (The Dutch or Amsterdam roede was 12.071 feet or 3.7674 meters.) Most farms were two lots or larger. The best land at the town center (Dorp) was held for the church. It is believed that the remaining lots were distributed by lottery, a common practice at that time. In its early years the town of Flatbush was divided into three parts: the northern part of the town was known as Steenraap or Stone Gathering because it was covered with small stones, probably the rubble from the glacial ridge; the southern end was called Rustenburgh, resting place, or borough; and the town center was Dorp. The Dorp was located at what is now the intersection of Flatbush and Church Avenues, the site of the First Reformed Dutch Church. In 1656, following hostilities on Staten Island, Flatbush was ordered to enclose the houses with a defensive palisade.

The Community at Home

The original settlers intended Flatbush to be a community of self-sufficient farmers (boers) and for many years it maintained itself without either mechanics or merchants. The usual division of labor was made up of men, including slaves, who did the farming, carpentry, leather-tanning, and shoe-making. In his *History of Flatbush* (1842), Thomas M. Strong, who served as minister of the First Reformed Dutch Church, explained that each man in Flatbush was "acquainted more or less, with some mechanical trade." According to him, "this was calculated to promote their domestic comfort, to render themselves useful to one or another, and to make them quite independent of extraneous aid."

The women, with the help of slaves, kept house, which was strenuous and demanding. They cooked, spun their own flax and wool, and made all necessary clothing. For example, before there were "dirt covers" or carpets, the bare floors were kept scrubbed and scoured by sanding. The process consisted of placing wet beach sand, which each family kept in sufficient supply, on the floor in small heaps. The sand was then allowed to dry. The following day the dry sand would be swept lightly across the floors and as it picked up dirt it left the floors white and clean. During the busy harvest and planting seasons the women often joined the men in the fields. Children, including slave children, were taught all the necessary skills for self-reliance at an early age. The work was hard but the fruit of their labor was reflected in their comfortably furnished and well-provisioned homes.

By the beginning of the eighteenth century a public brewery, located in the southern part of town, and at least two private breweries, had been established. At that time there was no prohibition against the use of alcoholic beverages, and beer and malt liquor were common. Once orchards were established and reached their maturity, cider became a substitute. Nevertheless, the public brewery stood until after the Revolution and one's share in it was considered a valuable asset. When it was sold, the proceeds were divided among the shareholders. According to Reverend Strong:

> [T]he public brewery was divided into fourteen shares, which were subdivided into halves and perchance quarters. These rights were apportioned to the several farms and considered appurtenant to them, and entitled the proprietors to the privilege of brewing in the establishment. These rights were disposed of by deed or testamentary devise. A will is in existence dated as late as 1773, devising the right of the testator in the brewery to his son; and several wills and deeds of early date are to be found, containing provisions to the same subject. So important was the right in this establishment at that time deemed by the proprietors.

From its earliest beginnings the community felt duty-bound to educate its young and to provide for its sick and its old. Before the church was built and before a minister arrived, laymen, known as "Krank-besoeckers," or "Ziekentroosters," gave comfort and care to the sick and aged. Their duties also included reading the Scriptures on Sunday. As early as 1658 or 1659, in conjunction with the church, the town had a schoolmaster who was responsible for both the secular and religious education of young boys and girls. The first of an unbroken line of schoolmasters was Adrian Hegeman, one of the original proprietors of Flatbush, who taught from 1659 to 1671.

The cultural life of the community was centered in the home and, even before it was a physical presence, the Reformed Dutch Church. An early community custom was "keeping schemeravond," a special family time. The word *schemeravond* means twilight, and every evening at dusk families, sometimes joined by neighbors, would gather around the hearth when it was cold, or on the front porch when it was warm, to discuss the days events and indulge their fondness for ghost stories or *sprookjes*. On those occasions when there were new arrivals from Holland, this evening time gave people a chance to catch up on the news from home.

The telling of ghost stories was apparently widely shared by the Dutch of New Netherlands. Washington Irving made it the centerpiece of his classic story *The Legend of Sleepy Hollow*, in which he adroitly captured the self-satisfaction and contentment of these farmers with their material success. The story was written in the late 1820s and, although it is set in a rustic village in New York's Hudson Valley, it is not difficult to believe that among the successful families on western Long Island life wasn't very much different. Nor is it hard to see how the complacency and material concerns of these farmers would allow the British to capture New Netherlands in 1664 without firing a shot, or later, on the eve of the Battle of Brooklyn, for the American patriots to mistrust them.

In *The Legend of Sleepy Hollow*, Irving introduces his audience to the wealthy farmer Baltrus Van Tassel, who could have just as easily been part of Flatbush's landed gentry. The old gentleman is described as "a perfect picture of a thriving, contented liberal hearted farmer, [who] seldom sent either his eyes or his thoughts beyond the boundaries of his own farm; but within those everything was snug, happy and well conditioned. He was satisfied with his wealth, but not proud of it, and piqued himself upon the hearty abundance, rather than the style in which he lived."

It is Van Tassel's wealth that the protagonist Ichabod Crane, a newcomer and Yankee from Connecticut, plots to possess. A casualty of his own greed and gullibility, Crane eventually gets his comeuppance in a late-night encounter with the headless horseman of Sleepy Hollow.

In *A History of Flatbush*, written a half century later, Gertrude Lefferts Vanderbilt took gentle umbrage at what she considered Irving's "ridicule" of her Hudson Valley landsmen. However, she acknowledged that all the old towns had their legends and *sprookjes* and regretted that so few of the Flatbush legends had been preserved.

Vanderbilt tells one story reminiscent of the ghostly pursuit of Ichabod Crane, albeit one with a happier ending, that was said to have happened in 1746. This story concerned a fateful trip by the old *domine* (minister) of the Flatbush Reformed Dutch Church. On the night in question the domine, on church business, had made what was then a long and difficult trip from the village of Flatbush to the village of Brooklyn. At the time both towns were sparsely populated and separated from each other by fields, forests, and the steep ridge of the terminal moraine; the road between the towns, especially at night, was lightly traveled. The domine, who missed the social evenings of Amsterdam, had been enjoying his visit and had not realized the lateness of the hour. Upon noticing the time, he quickly bid his host good night, lit his pipe, and mounted his horse for the long trip home. According to the story:

> [I]t was a moonless cloudy night. The road was darkened by the overreaching trees [that] seemed to nod to each other mysteriously overhead, and to whisper some secret across his path at the suggestion of the evening breeze. Through the narrow opening cut by the road he could see the faint line of the sky, but it gave no light down through this rift of forest. . . . [A]s he passed on the woods closed around him and the night seemed darker than before. The hill crossed he descend[ed] to the place where the road led through a low and marshy district. An uncanny spot was this that now lay before him. Old legends placed evil spirits and ghosts in such shadowy corners. Even to this day a damper air strikes the traveler as he turns down to this hollow; a darker shadow rests upon the road here, and a mistiness and dampness from the ponds beyond make the place miasmatic and unhealthy.

This area, the setting of another *sprookje*, was said to be the place where Satan had once danced. An imprint of his cloven foot on a stone proved the tale. Ironically, much later, on November 1, 1918, this haunted spot became the scene of the Malborne Street wreck, the worst subway accident in New York City history. Returning to the eighteenth century and to the plight of the domine:

> As he approached this spot the domine tightened the reigns and strove to encourage his steed into some gait quicker than the usual pace of a ministerial horse. He thrust his pipe into his pocket and patted the neck of the animal. In grateful acknowledgement it started off into a brisk trot. A pleasant breeze springing up at the same time induced the traveler to hope that this haunted region might prove even an agreeable change from the stony hilltop. Suddenly he was startled by a faint light which seemed to follow him at a close and equal rate. Vainly he looked around; no object was perceptible. A vigorous application of the whip roused the horse to increase his speed, but there was no diminution of the light.
>
> The good minister urged his horse to go faster and faster, but he could not escape the light. He raced along the road through Flatbush, pursued by the ghostly light. He sped past the familiar houses and yet he could not escape his pursuer. Finally, utterly exhausted, he was no longer able to urge his horse on. By instinct the animal turned in at the open gate and stopped at the back stoop of his house. It was then he saw his reflection in his candlelit window. What he saw—to his great relief—was that his riding clothes—the voluminous garments that were the style of the day—had suffered severely from contact with fire.

Nevertheless, Vanderbilt suggests: "The half extinguished pipe thrust hastily in his pocket might account for the result." But, she adds, perhaps with a sly wink:

> it is well known that ghosts are opposed to knowledge as deadly to their very existence; and as the old Domine was a very learned man, we see good reason why they should be particularly exasperated against him. We therefore take a bold stand, and agree with those who at the time did not hesitate to assert as their belief that the Domine was pursued with vindictive zeal by a fiery phantom from the Clove in the Hollow . . .

The Early Homesteads

Among the few surviving Dutch homesteads in Brooklyn from the period before 1800 are the Pieter Claesen Wyckoff House (1652), the oldest of the structures; the Hendrick I. Lott House (1720); the Wyckoff-Bennett House (1766); the Lefferts Homestead (reconstructed 1777–1783); the Jan Martense Schenck House (*c.* 1675); and the house of his grandson Nickolas Schenck built about one hundred years later, *c.* 1775. The last two houses were removed form their original sites in Flatlands and rebuilt inside the Brooklyn Museum of Art where they are open to the public. Of all the remaining houses, only the Lefferts Homestead was located in Flatbush. And in 1918 in order to preserve it, that house had to be moved to Prospect from its original location at 563 Flatbush Avenue. The other houses were located in Flatlands. Nevertheless, combined, the stories of these houses and the families that inhabited them are central to understanding life in the sparsely populated Dutch towns of seventeenth- and eighteenth-century Booklyn and the role of the town of Flatbush. Although there were periodic disputes between these small farming communities, until the end of the American Revolution, with the exception of Gravesend, there were no significant lifestyle or cultural distinctions.

It is almost serendipitous that any buildings from the past would survive in New York, a city driven by change and development. Although today New Yorkers do fight valiantly to protect architecture of historical significance, until the late twentieth century New York generally placed little value on protecting its historic buildings. Thus, the circumstances of the survival of these few old Dutch homesteads and their present condition is specific to each house. If there is a common denominator, it is that with one exception (the Lefferts homestead) all of the above buildings are located in places that were peripheral to the expansion of public transportation and early development.

These buildings are among the few intact domestic structures that are typical of Dutch architecture that was distinct from the "boxlike" architecture in neighboring English settlements. In his book, *Dutch by Design*, Kevin L. Slayton, Curator of the Decorative Arts at the Brooklyn Museum of Art, described the Jan Martense House (*c.* 1675) as, "[a] simple but well-crafted two-room wooden structure organized around a central chimney with a loft for storage above, it is constructed along a typical Dutch (or more generally, Continental) framing plan." The historian David Steven Cohen, as quoted in Slayton, provides a generic description of the "continental frame:"

> Unlike the boxlike English frame, the continental frame resembles a series of goal posts known as H-bents, each consisting of two vertical posts connected by a large anchor beam and reinforced by diagonal corner braces. Atop the posts on either side of the H-bents run horizontal plates, which support the widely spaced rafters of the pitched roof. The paired rafters are reinforced by collar beams and joined at the peak by mortise and tenon joints; . . . there is no ridge pole.

In addition to the design of the houses, the stories of the families who occupied them epitomize the web of familiar connections that wove the towns together. And finally, the survival of these buildings in Flatlands, but not in Flatbush, is illustrative of development in Brooklyn. Because of its location at the center of Kings County, Flatbush had always been the meeting place and market town, but it only began to significantly differentiate itself from the neighboring towns after the Revolutionary War. With improvements in public transportation, particularly the building of the Brooklyn-Flatbush & Coney Island Railroad in 1878 (which later became the Brighton line of the BMT subway) and the arrival of the electric trolley in 1890, Flatbush grew exponentially. These improvements made Flatbush an accessible and desirable location to live. In 1894, after Flatbush was annexed by the City of Brooklyn, new taxes destroyed the feasibility of farming, forcing many families to subdivide their land and sell it to real estate developers. Those early twentieth-century developers would totally change the face of Flatbush. Flatlands, on the other hand, was peripheral to the pressures of urbanization that were driving Flatbush. Its last farms disappeared after World War II.

The Pieter Claesen-Wyckoff House, located at 5816 Clarendon Road (corner of Ralph Avenue) is the earliest remaining wood structure in New York state. The American Institute of Architects, in its *Guide to New York City Architecture* (2000), aptly describes the house and its surroundings as, "A lonely ancestor in a neatly fenced park, marooned in these industrial precincts. A vast lawn and minimal trees surround this modest place, which remembers the New Netherlands with its handsome eaves and shingled body."

The earliest wing of the house was built in 1652. It was one room and housed Claesen, his wife, and their eleven children. When the east wing was added between 1730 and 1750, the original house with its great open-hearth fireplace became the kitchen of the larger dwelling. In 1819 the roof was raised to provide additional space and the center hall was added. Until it was sold in 1902, Claesen descendants continuously occupied the house.

Sixty years later, in 1962, the Wyckoff House Association, made up of Claesen's descendants, repurchased the house. Shortly thereafter in 1965, it became the first building designated a New York City Landmark under the new city landmarks law; it is also listed in the National Register of Historic Places. In 1970 the Wyckoff Association donated the house to New York City. After extensive restoration it was opened to the public in 1982 as a house-museum. The association continues to play a role in its management and has donated back to the house many of the original objects that are on display.

The story of Pieter Claesen, who arrived in New Netherlands as an illiterate, indentured servant and rose to great wealth and prominence, is one of the earliest "American" success stories. It is also indicative of the diverse populations that peopled New Netherlands. By contrast, the English settlements tended to be more homogeneous.

Born in Norden in the Holy Roman Empire (now East Friesland, Germany), Claesen as a young man faced a bleak future. Hoping to better his fortunes he set off for Amsterdam, and his ultimate destination New Netherlands. In April 1637, after a difficult voyage, he arrived in New Amsterdam. From there he traveled to Rensselearswyck, the Hudson Valley estate of the wealthy Dutch merchant Kiliean van Rensselear, where he served for six years as an indentured servant. After completing his service he married Grietie van Nes, the daughter of Cornelis Hendricksen van Nes, a wealthy farmer and respected member of the Rensselearwyck community. Recognizing that advancement would be limited on the Rensselear manor, the couple left for Nieuw Amersfoort in order to take advantage of the Dutch West India Company offer of free farmland.

In Nieuw Amersfoort, Claesen managed Governor Stuyvasant's farm and in his own right became a successful farmer and one of the town's wealthiest men. He also rose to great prominence in the community when in 1655 his friend, Governor Stuyvesant, appointed him a town *schepen* (magistrate). He held that post until 1665, stepping down after the English conquered New Netherlands and replaced the schepens with a board of overseers. At that time too the English ordered all families to take a surname. Since surnames were not part of Dutch tradition, Claesen constructed the name Wyckoff. It is believed that all Wyckoffs today, despite the various spellings of the name, are descendants of Claesen and are related to each other.

As house-museums, both the Claesen Wyckoff House and the Lefferts Homestead operate interactively, offering a "hands on" experience of the past. These houses are used to educate the public, especially children, and provide activities that recall and teach the old arts and crafts. At the Claesen House, which is more out of the way and less heavily visited, the events are planned to mark specific seasonal occasions. The Lefferts Homestead, located in Prospect Park between the zoo and carousel, attracts over 40,000 visitors per year. It is one the most heavily used of the city's house museums and maintains an ongoing program of planned activities. Operated since 1993 by the Prospect Park Alliance, it is specifically organized as a children's historic house museum, interpreting life in the farming community of Flatbush as it was experienced by Dutch, African, and Native-American children in the early 1800s. As described by the Prospect Park Alliance:

> Visitors to the Homestead play with traditional tools, toys and games and have the unique chance to engage in seasonal farm activities. Families also participate in craft activities such as candle making, sewing, butter churning, and making fire with flint and steel. Special weekend programs follow the seasonal patterns of rural life: from spring flax planting, wool washing, garden planting and Pinkster Day (a re-creation of the historic Dutch- and African-American celebration of the Pentecost), to the lazy days

of storytelling in mid-summer, and ending with the early Harvest Fair and Winter Festival.

The Lefferts family was among the first to settle in Flatbush. Pietersen Janse Hagewout arrived from North Holland with his family aboard *De Bonte Koe* (the Spotted Cow) in 1660. however, his son, Leffert Pietersen (1650–1704), is considered the founding ancestor. He married Abigail Van Nuyse, Daughter of Aucke Janse, the founder of what would become another prominent Flatbush family.

The earliest record of Leffert's family-owned land is in a deed signed by Governor Stuyvesant and dated 1661. The land was located at the northern end of the town on the east side of Flatbush Avenue, what today would be the area of Flatbush Avenue and Maple Street. By 1676 the Lefferts family land and other property was assessed at £104, a considerable sum for that time. By 1683 Leffert Pietersen had increased the wealth to £174/10. His son Pieter (1680–1774) married Eyte Suydam (d. 1777) of a prominent Flatbush family. From 1737 to 1772 Pieter served as county treasurer, the first of a long line of family members who would take an active role in public service.

In 1767 Pieter sold his Flatbush homestead to his son Jan (John) for £1,400. Jan (1719–1776) married Sarah Martense (1727–1762) of the large landholding Martense family and upon her death he married Lemmetje Vanderbilt (1720–1782) of the equally prominent Flatbush Vanderbilt family. Jan had a distinguished record of public service. He served as judge of the Court of Sessions and Common Pleas from 1751 to 1761, and as a county judge from 1761 to 1770. He was town clerk of Flatbush from 1773 to 1776, and a delegate to the Provincial Congress.

His son Pieter (1753–1791), following in his father's and grandfather's footsteps, had a distinguished career of public service. During the Revolutionary War he served as a lieutenant of the militia of Flatbush. Afterwards he was elected a state senator and later became a judge on the County Court of Sessions and Common Pleas. In 1788 he was one of the delegates to the state convention to ratify the Constitution of the United States.

On August 26, 1776, the eve of the Battle of Brooklyn, 550 Pennsylvania riflemen attacked the Hessian encampment in Flatbush. During the fighting several homes occupied by the British, including the Lefferts farmhouse, were set afire. After the war Pieter, who was one of the richest men in Flatbush, rebuilt the house. His household at the time consisted of eight family members and twelve slaves.

Eight generations of Lefferts had lived in the house before the family donated it to the City of New York in 1918. In order to save the house from the wrecker's ball, it was moved several blocks to its present location in Prospect Park. Architecturally, the house has been described as "combin[ing] Dutch Colonial architecture with early Federal details. It has a bell-shaped gambrel roof, front and back porches with slender columns, and symmetrically arranged rooms along a central hall."

Another of the important remaining Dutch farmhouses is the Hendrick I. Lott House at 1940 East 36th Street. The Lott family too was one of the largest landholders in the area with holdings in Flatbush and Flatlands. With the Wyckoffs, they owned a broad swath of the East Flatbush–Flatlands area from Kings Highway to Jamaica Bay several miles to the south. Like Flatbush Avenue, Kings Highway began as an Indian trail that traversed the area from east to west. Today it is an important thoroughfare that winds through southern and eastern Brooklyn. The original lands of the Claesen-Wyckoff farm, the Hendrick I. Lott farm, and the Wyckoff-Bennett homestead all bordered on it.

Peter Lott, the family patriarch, arrived in Flatbush in 1652. His origins are not known. According to a family history written in 1858 by Jeremiah Lott, the family was originally from England, and through intermarriage acquired its Dutch identity. Other histories say that Peter Lott was born in Holland. Regardless of where he was born, by 1685 Peter had attained sufficient prominence in the community to be named by Lieutenant Governor Dongan a patentee of the town of Flatbush on the English patent that replaced the old Dutch charter. Other early Lotts who achieved high office included Peter's son Engelbert (1654–1726), who was appointed high sheriff of Kings County in 1698 by Richard, earl of Bellamont, governor of the Province of New York. In 1743 Abraham Lott (1684–1754), one of Engelbert's sons, was elected to a seven-year term as representative from Kings County to the state colonial legislature. Re-elected to a second term in 1750, Abraham died in office four years later.

The Lott family, like the Lefferts, provides a good example of the web of connections through marriage among the prominent families of the various towns. Abraham (of Flatbush), Peter Lott's grandson, married Catherina Hegeman (1691–1741), the daughter of one of the old families of Flatlands. Their second son, another Engelbert (1719–1779), who married Martije Ditmas from an established Flatbush family, became the principal land surveyor of Kings County and was one of the judges in the Court of Common Pleas. Finally, Johannes E. Lott (1746–1811), from Flatbush, the eldest son of Engelbert and Martije, was selected one of the six delegates from Kings County to attend the provisional Congress held in New York City in 1776. In 1784 he was elected to the New York State Assembly and was later appointed first surrogate of Kings County. He too married into two landholding families. First he married Adriantje Vooheries (1746–1773) of Gravesend, and upon her death he married Catherine Vanderbilt (1757–1840) of Flatbush.

Johannes Lott (1692–1775), the grandfather of Hendrick I. Lott, purchased the land on which the Hendrick I. Lott House stands from Coert Voorheis in 1719 for £2,100. Johannes and his wife Antje Folkersen built a small "saltbox" type house where they lived for the rest of their lives. They also continued to acquire property, extending their holdings to Jamaica Bay. Upon Lott's death, the farm passed to his son Johannes Jr. (1721–1792), who left the house and farm to Hendrick I. (1760–1840), one of his sons. In 1792 Hendrick married Mary Brownjohn, daughter of Dr. Thomas Brownjohn and Elizabeth Campbell Brownjohn. The Brownjohns were prominent New York landholders. Mary was the sister of Elizabeth, the wife of Hendrick's brother Christopher. At the time, marriages between the siblings of one family to siblings in another family were quite common.

In 1800 Hendrick I. Lott built the large house in the Dutch Colonial style and incorporated his grandfather's original 1720 house as the kitchen wing. At that time his farm was more than 200 acres, extending to the Strome Kill (later known as Garretson's Creek or Mill Pond) on Brooklyn's south shore. By the end of the nineteenth century, however, most of the land had been subdivided and sold for development. Writing in praise of the house in 1909, about one hundred years after it was built, Charles Andrew Ditmas, himself a scion of the old Flatbush family, noted that "the original shingle roof still protect[ed] the house and the house [was] still standing firm as a rock, ready to stand another hundred years, if her owners still will it. It is hoped that they will because where can you find a home of better, purer nobler design."

Today the house sits on about three-quarters of an acre, in the middle of a city block, in Marine Park, a residential neighborhood of small attached and semi-attached homes that were built in the 1920s and 1930s. Although all the other houses on the block face east, the Lott House has not been moved and it still faces south. Until 1989 the house was the home of Ella and Anna Suydam, the last Lott descendants to live there. After their deaths the house fell onto hard times. An effort to preserve and save it was spearheaded by many of its Marine Park neighbors. In October 1989, over the objections of the then current owner, and with strong support from the Marine Park community, it was designated an New York City landmark by the New York City Landmark's Preservation Commission. In making the designation the commission stated:

> [T]he Hendrick I. Lott House is a rare surviving example of a Dutch colonial house in Brooklyn and one of the finest of the type; built in 1800 by Hendrick I. Lott, the house incorporates a section of the 1720 house built by his grandfather Johannes Lott; that with the exception of portions of the Pieter Claesen Wyckoff House, this is the earliest surviving eighteenth century fabric in any of the Dutch Colonial houses in Brooklyn, that among the traditional characteristics of the Hendrick I. Lott House are its southern orientation, the gambrel roof with a spring eave forming the roof of the columned porch, the end chimneys, and the shingled siding; that the symmetrical composition of the house is unparalleled in any other example of Dutch Colonial architecture in Brooklyn; that the house has an extraordinary degree of integrity; that it also has the rare distinction of retaining its original orientation on its original site with sufficient surrounding property to give some sense of its original setting; and that until very recently the house has been occupied by descendants of the Lott family which had established itself in Brooklyn in 1652.

An article in the *New York Times* on December 28, 2002 quoted Catherine Lott, a descendant who recalled a visit she had made to her cousins many years earlier. During the visit, Lott told the *Times*, she was taken upstairs by her cousins and led into a large closet. Behind the clothes rack and the stacks of hatboxes they showed her a small, carefully concealed door that was cut into the back wall. The small room on the other side of the door, according to Lott family legend and seemingly confirmed by recent research, was a "safe house" on the Underground Railroad. "It was mind blowing"

Catherine Lott told the *Times*. Then her cousins swore her to secrecy, "All the old relatives that I knew had this interesting moral code," she explained. "[I]f something was secret in the 1880s it was always a secret." According to the article, "Census records from 1803 show that the Lotts had twelve slaves. By the end of the decade, the Lotts had freed their slaves and apparently hired them back as paid workers, thereby becoming one of the first families in the area to free their slaves. This had led historians to speculate tht the Lotts were abolitionists." Catherine Lott seemed to confirm this to the *Times*, recalling that her "father's generation remember[ed] being able to see the water [Jamaica Bay] from the upstairs bedroom windows. The thinking was that the ships came quietly in the night to the shore and the people who were part of the Underground Railroad would shepherd the slaves into the house."

By contrast, the Wyckoff-Bennett House, on East 22nd Street near Kings Highway, has been continuously lived in, well cared for, and loved since 1766. It is thought that the first owner, Hendrick H. Wyckoff, built it in 1766 because the date was carved into an original beam in an old barn. In 1835 it was purchased by Cornelius Bennett of Gowanus, a descendant of William Adriaense Bennet (he spelled his name with one "t") who in 1636 had made the first land purchase in Gowanus. Included in the house purchase were the barn, slave quarters, and about one hundred acres of land. He also gained possession of pew 62 in the Gravesend Dutch Reformed Church.

At the beginning of the twentieth century most of the farm was sold to the Wood Harmon Company for development. At about the same time the city was opening streets along a grid. This caused the loss of the barn and slave quarters and also made it necessary to change the orientation of the house from facing south to facing west so that it would fit into the city block. At the same time the house was raised to allow the installation of a furnace, and the original stoop was replaced with a long front porch. It is believed that the largest trees and the grape vine date from this period. It was designated a New York City Landmark in 1968.

The last Bennett to occupy the house was Gertrude Ryder-Bennett (1901–1982), a writer and poet. Her husband, Reverend Frank Curtis Williams, was pastor of the South Reformed Church of Brooklyn. Bennett-Williams wrote two books about her house. The first, *Living in a Landmark* (1980), is a personal memoir and a biography of the house. The second book, *The Hessian Lieutenant Left His Name* (1976), is written in verse and tells the story of Lieutenant M. Bach, a Hessian mercenary who occupied the house during the Revolutionary War and was one of two enemy officers who scratched his name onto a windowpane. In the 1980s, after the death of Gertrude Bennett-Williams, the house was sold. It is occupied by a private family and is not open to the public.

The two houses on display at the Brooklyn Museum of Art stood about a mile and a half apart from each other. They belonged to Jan Martense Schenck (*c.* 1675; reconstructed at the museum to how it looked in 1730) and to his grandson Nicholas Schenck (*c.* 1775). Each house was dismantled, removed from its original site, and reconstructed from its same materials in the museum. The newer and larger of the houses, the Nicholas Schenck House, was acquired by the museum in 1929 and the

Jan Martense Schenck House may have been saved from the wrecker's ball when it was acquired many years later in 1952. It was not until 1963–1964 that the house was actually reconstructed at the museum.

These houses interpret the home life of a successful Long Island farmer in the seventeenth and eighteenth centuries respectively, and they provide a comparison of how life had changed for the milieu over a period of one hundred years. Nevertheless, museum curator Kevin L. Slayton points out, "it is never really possible to recreate the living dynamics of a specific room as they existed in the past when the room was in use." To recreate period rooms the museum relied on artifacts, government records, wills, deeds, images, written descriptions, and in the case of the Jan Martense Schenck House, eighteenth-century paintings depicting similar homes in Holland.

Typical of its time, the Jan Martense Schenck House was one and a half stories tall. It was built with low ceilings in order to preserve the heat, which was provided by a central fireplace. The fireplace, characteristic of most houses of this period, was usually sufficiently wide to allow all members of the family a seat at the fire. The chimney was large enough to hang meat in order to smoke it, the common practice at the time. One of the early methods of cleaning these chimneys was described by Gertrude Lefferts Vanderbilt:

> In earlier years little colored boys used to ascend the chimney from the open fireplace with scraper and brush. Poor little fellows! Theirs was a hard life. It had, however, this alleviation, the fact that they soon outgrew the possibility of its continuance, for only small children could creep up the chimney. When they reached the top, they were expected to thrust out their heads, like chimney swallows, and to sing their melancholy song from that height. This was the announcement that they had really reached the top before they began their descent. . . . A man generally accompanied these little sweeps; and it was he who hired them and to whom the money for their work was to be paid; but they were often very cruelly treated by their employers and in this country, as well as in England, this manner of sweeping chimneys was finally forbidden by law.

Typically the main floor of the early houses had two rooms, a north room and a south room, both of which had a fireplace and were not differentiated by function. Above them was a storage loft; there was also a cellar for laying in provisions. The cellar, according to Vanderbilt, was carefully built to be cool in the summer and warm in the winter. It was usually constructed of unhewn stone, with either a brick or earthen floor. In order to keep them clean, the cellars were white-washed twice a year.

The furnishings and utensils in the museum houses are authentic to the time and place, but they do not necessarily belong to the particular house. Another example of the curatorial process seen in the house is the inclusion of curtained cupboard beds. These beds were widely used in Holland and can be seen in many eighteenth-century

Dutch paintings. However, according to Slayton, the cupboard beds placed in the north wall are "almost entirely on speculation alone, for there is no undisputed physical evidence of the use of such beds in American houses."

Styles of domestic architecture changed significantly in the one hundred years between the building of the Jan Martense Schenck House and The Nicholas Schenck House. The latter represents the architectural transformation that was taking place in the population as it adopted an American identity. The new domestic architectural style—a mixture of English and Dutch elements—was popularly known as "Dutch Colonial." Slayton calls this building style that was typical of eighteenth- and early nineteenth-century homes in Kings County "quintessentially American." This style of house differed from contemporary Dutch houses of the time located in Manhattan and in the Hudson River Valley. In those areas the houses were made of stone. On Long Island the houses were shingle. According to Slayton:

> When [the house] stood on site it presented a classic Dutch Colonial profile, with gently sloping gambrel roof and flaring, overhanging eaves. There was a large opening high in one gable end so that material could be hoisted into the loft for storage, and in front were a stoop, or porch, and a Dutch door that had its original upper panel replaced by a stationary transom sometime around 1880. The house was covered with shingles, which along with clapboards were used on Long Island and in parts of New Jersey where soil was sandy and stone was scarce. . . . Inside the house as it is now installed in the Museum, the customary low ceilings with exposed beams supporting wide plank boards are still visible. The stair hall is wainscoted with a simple sheathing of flat boards and the fireplace ends of both the parlor and dining room are paneled—a stylistic feature borrowed from the English."

As one entered the Nickolas Schenck House through the front door, one stepped into a center hall that extended to the rear of the house. Opening on to the hall was the dining room on the left (as one faced the rear of the house) and the living room to the right. Toward the rear of the hall was the staircase to the second floor. In the rear of the house, also opening onto the hall, were two bedrooms. Upstairs there were three additional bedrooms and storage space.

The Church

Because of Flatbush's central location—it shared part of its border with each of the towns of western Long Island—it became the seat of government and religion. It was also an important market town for western Long Island. Beginning in 1658 courts were conducted in Flatbush and the public officers, including the court officials (secretary or town clerk, sheriff, and schoolmaster) resided there. For a short time after the British conquest of New Netherlands in 1664 the seat of government was shifted to the English town of Gravesend, but in 1685 it was returned to Flatbush where it remained until 1832 when a fire gutted the courthouse.

Flatbush

In 1654 Governor General Stuyvesant ordered that a Reformed Dutch Church be constructed at the center of the town, at what are now the major cross streets of Flatbush and Church Avenues. To oversee its construction, he appointed a three-man committee consisting of Domine (Reverend) Megapolensis of New Amsterdam, and Jan Snedicor and Jan Strijker, both of Flatbush. The church was probably made of wood and as directed by Stuyvesant, designed in the form of a cross. It was sixty-five feet long, and at its widest twenty-eight feet across. Its ceiling was fourteen feet high. The rear of the church was reserved for the minister's dwelling. The deacons' book shows that the collections for the building fund began on the first Sabbath of January 1655 and continued weekly. The final cost of building was approximately 4,637 guilders (about $1,800)—a substantial sum for the day. The funds were raised by voluntary subscription locally, as well as in New Amsterdam and in the Dutch villages along the Hudson, including Fort Orange. (See box on page 65.) Governor Stuyvesant also contributed 400 guilders to the construction. Nevertheless, the church was 800 guilders in debt when it was completed in September 1660.

The general organization of the Reformed Dutch Church consisted of congregations of individual communicants who were guided by their minister (domine), who preached the word of God and administered the sacraments, the elders (*ouderlingen*), and the deacons. The elders and deacons were generally drawn from the town elite. At the local level the ministers, elders, and deacons formed consistories (*kerkenraden*). The several consistories of a region formed a class. Until 1772, more than one hundred years after the British had captured New Netherlands, all the Reformed Dutch Churches in Kings County were administered from Holland by the Classis of Amsterdam, which provided the ministers and was the final arbiter of all church-related questions. In 1772 there was a reorganization and independent classes were established. Until then the churches in the five Dutch towns of Brooklyn were treated as one consistory. In his *History of the Town of Flatbush*, published in 1842, Thomas M. Strong, minister of the Dutch Reformed Church of Flatbush from 1822 until his death in 1861, described the arrangement: "On Long Island, each town had its own consistory, or bench of church officers; but all the churches in Kings county [Brooklyn] were combined, and constituted one charge, for the period of about 150 years. Their ministers were colleagues; preached in turn at all the churches; and drew their salaries in certain fixed proportions from several congregations. The place of their residence was Flatbush."

Prior to building the church and the arrival of its first domine Johannes Theodorus Polhemus in 1654, formal religious services in Flatbush and the other towns were dependent upon infrequent visits from New Amsterdam ministers. On occasion, families would travel to New Amsterdam for services. Ordinarily, however, the farmers would attend local "informal" services presided over by laymen, usually the schoolmaster, and the ziekentrooster or krank-besoecker, the comforters of the sick.

The centrality of Flatbush made it the ideal site for a church that was intended to serve the Dutch towns. According to the plan, Sunday morning services would be held in Flatbush and afternoon services would alternate between Brooklyn and Flatlands. In practice, the plan was less than satisfactory and it was not long before both Brooklyn and Flatlands, respectively, petitioned Stuyvesant for permission to build a church of their own. In 1660 Brooklyn separated from the church of Flatbush. Flatlands continued the relationship until 1665, one year after the Dutch lost control of the New Netherlands colonies. In that year Flatlands demanded Sunday morning services be preached alternately at Flatbush and Flatlands. The decision of the British Governor Richard Nicolls favored Flatlands.

In 1654 Domine Johannes Theodorus Polhemus, the first minister to take up residence on western Long Island, arrived in Flatbush from his previous ministry in Brazil. He served the congregation for twenty-two years until his death in 1676. In 1656 residents of Flatbush, Brooklyn, and Flatlands informed Governor Peter Stuyvesant that they were satisfied with Polhemus and agreed to pay him a salary of approximately $416.66 per year. Nevertheless, for Polhemus it was a difficult ministry. First he was caught in the conflicts between the towns. Travel was not easy, and became increasingly difficult as he aged. Nevertheless, the towns expected him to provide the full service, including the traditional long sermons, and when he did not he was severely criticized. Furthermore, not everybody wanted to pay for the minister, and he often had difficulty collecting his salary. Early in his ministry he even had problems gaining comfortable accommodations for himself and his family. These matters became the subject of an ongoing correspondence that Polhemus and his wife maintained with Governor Stuyvesant.

For example, on December 14, 1656, Polhemus wrote to Stuyvesant to complain that lumber sent by the governor to complete his house had been used for other purposes. The minister was distressed that his house was still open and that he and his family was exposed to the winter.

Stuyvesant, in a letter to the magistrates of Midwout dated December 21, 1656, ordered them to uphold their agreement and provide suitable accommodations for the minister and his family:

> Honorable, Dear, Faithful.
> When you were in Breuckelen at the house of Albert Cornelissen it was agreed in parting by mutual consent and approbation of yourselves and the other delegates from the villages of Breuckelen and Amesfoort, that you should together make an estimate of the funds, out of which the preacher Domine Polheym [*sic*], was to be paid and placed above want and report it to us and the Council within eight days. As this time has passed and we are not yet informed of the result, we have deemed it necessary to remind you of it through the Schout [sheriff] and this open letter, that you fulfill our promise; else we shall be compelled by our official position and duties to take steps and give such orders and provide for such means that the Minister be duly paid and placed above want. The said Domine Polheym, who was then present, complained further of the uninhabitable state and inconvenience of his dwelling house, which has yet neither ceiling nor wainscoting so that he and

> his family are compelled to sleep on the floor. The winter being imminent, this is unbearable and improper, and in order to remedy it we sent you for the ceiling and wainscoting of the house one hundred hemlock planks which parties deputed by you received and carried to my brother's-in-law Backer's house. I am however credibly informed now, that the said boards have not been used for the purposes intended by us, but that the Commissaries disposed of them privately according to their pleasure; for instance, so I am told, twenty four have been given to the hired man of Jan Evertsen; six ordered to be cut up for benches, seventeen given by Jan Snedicker to the Swartwouts so that the boards disappeared here and there, while nothing was done to finish the Minister's house, which is most urgent to do, the winter being so near at hand. We command therefore herewith, that the boards be brought together again upon receipt hereof, and put to their proper use and to none other, as we have ordered. If you fail herein, we shall take proper measures; where upon relying we commend you all with the usual greetings to God's protection and remain.
> P. Stuyvesant.

On the same day, December 21, 1656, Polhemus petitioned Stuyvesant for a salary advance in order to pay a note on land he had purchased from Cornells Aerssen. Polhemus blamed his inability to pay the note on the difficulties of getting his salary paid. A few weeks later the magistrates, in order to raise the money needed to pay Polhemus, petitioned Stuyvesant for permission to levy a land tax and power to enforce it. Their request was granted.

Actual construction of the church began in 1658 and was completed in 1660. A Minute of the Council of New Amsterdam dated September 30, 1660, indicated that Domine Polhemus and Jan Strycker, elder and church master, had appeared before the council to ask that the Dutch West India Company provide a window and some additional funds. At the time they presented an accounting showing that they had raised fl. 3,437.12 for the church building and that they still owed fl. 624. (Guilders and florins were equal to each other and herein are used interchangeably.) Specifically, the debt was owed to Jacob Lourens, carpenter, fl. 230; Isaac Foreest, for nails, fl. 117; Tyde Syricks, mason, fl. 215; Sander, the skipper, for freight of boards, fl. 81; and Aucke Jansen, carpenter for outside work, fl. 100. It also showed that the church was owed fl. 119 by Claes Notelear. The council agreed to provide a window and an additional 400 florins "when the treasury had the funds." In March 1661 the two men returned to ask for additional funds to cover fl. 190 of additional debt. The council agreed to pay half the amount "when there was money in the treasury."

A Minute of the Council at New Amsterdam dated January 4, 1663, notes that having completed the church building and retiring its debt, Polhemus and Stryker came before it asking to be relieved of their duties as church masters. The council granted the petition and authorized the town magistrates to nominate two persons for each position. The governor general would then select the new church masters from the dual list.

Domine Polhemus died on June 8, 1676. He had served the Church of Flatbush, which at that time also included the churches of Brooklyn, Flatlands, and New Utrecht. An obituary, found among the papers of the Brooklyn Church, noted his passing:

> It has pleased the Almighty God, to remove from this world of care and trouble, our worthy and beloved pastor, Johannes Polhemus, to the abode of peace and happiness in his heavenly kingdom: by which, our Church is deprived of his pious instructions, godly example and evangelical ministrations, particularly in the administration of the holy sacrament of the Lord's Supper.

On August 29, 1676 the Reverend William Van Nieuwenhuysen of Brooklyn wrote to the Classis of Amsterdam requesting a new minister for Flatbush. More than a year later, in September 1677, the Reverend Casparus Van Zuren arrived in Flatbush. He served the church until 1685 when he returned to Holland. The third minister, Reverend Rudolphus Varick, served from 1685 to 1694. He was followed by the Reverend Wilhemus Lupundus, who served from 1694 to his death in 1701 or 1702. There are few records of these ministries.

In 1698, during the ministry of Reverend Lupundus, it was decided to replace the old wooden church with a new stone church to be built at the same location. A building committee composed of Captain Daniel Polhemus, Captain Aries Vanderbilt, Adrian Ryers, Rem Remsen, and Rem Aertson was appointed. The new building, which faced east, was larger than the previous one and cost about £15,728. The pulpit was placed in the center of the west wall facing the front door. The Elders bench was on the right and the deacons bench was on the left. Men and women sat separately. The men sat in a continuous pew along the wall, which was divided into twenty compartments; the women sat on chairs arranged in seven different rows or blocks and every family had one or more chairs in one of these blocks. The new church also provided for interments under the church. People who wanted the vaults paid a steep price, upwards of £4 per adult. All ministers who died after 1701 were buried there.

The next ministers to serve were the Reverends Bernardus Freeman and Vincentius Antonides. In 1702, shortly after the death of Reverend Lupundus, representatives from the towns of Flatbush, Bushwick, Flatlands, and New Utrecht asked the British Governor Lord Cornbury for permission to recruit Reverend Freeman from his ministry in Schenectady, New York. At first Lord Cornbury refused the request, but later relented. Nevertheless, according to historian Henry R. Stiles, author of *A History of the City of Brooklyn* (1867), other church elders found the act of seeking permission from the British governor, and thereby allowing him to "interfere" in church affairs, offensive. They rejected the appointment of Reverend Freeman. Instead, they wrote to the Classis of Amsterdam and asked them to send a minister. On December 26, 1705 Reverend Freeman was given his commission from Governor Lord Cornbury to minister to the Dutch congregations in Kings County. He was installed at the church in New Utrecht, but with the mandate of ministering to all the congregations. Simultaneously in January

1706 the Reverend Vincentius Antonides arrived from Holland and was installed at the church in Flatbush.

For more than thirteen years a divisive battle that engaged four British governors raged within the church and among its congregants over control. Finally in late 1714 a convention of delegates from the various churches of Kings County agreed to put aside their differences and recognize both Reverend Freeman and Reverend Antonides as their ministers. The two ministers worked together and established the practice for a dual ministry that continued until 1822 when Reverend Thomas M. Strong assumed the pulpit. When Reverend Freeman died in 1741 he was followed by the Reverend Johannes Arondeus in 1742. Reverend Antonides died in 1744 and was replaced by Reverend Ulpianus Van Sinderen, who served until 1784 when he retired. During the American Revolution, Reverend Van Sinderen was a strong supporter of the patriots' cause. Reverend Androneus died in 1755 and was succeeded by Reverend Anthony Curenius, who died shortly after being called. His successor, the Reverend Johannes Casparus Rubel, was called in 1759 and continued in office until 1784 when he was censured and expelled for his activities on behalf of the British during the American Revolution.

In 1775, the year before the American Revolution, the congregation decided to remodel the church building; the chairs were removed and sixty-four pews were installed. John Bennan, Thomas Lane, Isaac Martense, Adrian Martense, and Vincent Antonides were the carpenters, and William Post was the painter. The renovation cost £290.16.9. In order to raise the money, the pews were sold for £190.4.6. According to common practice they were distributed by lottery. Along the east wall, facing the alter, there were two galleries divided by the doors. One gallery was occupied by whites, the other by people of color; the benches below the galleries were free and usually occupied by visitors. The bell rope hung down the center of the church and during the Revolution was pulled often to sound alarms.

Design flaws in the church, however, had caused substantial damage to it that could not be repaired or ignored. In August 1793, the people of Flatbush, at a public meeting held at the church, agreed a new building was needed. A building committee, consisting of the five trustees of the church and five commissioners was named: Cornelius Vanderveer, John Bennem, Johannes J. Lott, Peter Stryker, John Vanderveer, John Vanderbilt, Hendrick H. Suydam, Johannes E. Lott, John Williamson, and Adrian Martense. They hired Thomas Fardon as the architect and master builder. Simeon Back, Frederic Cleaveland, Abijah Baldwin, and Gideon Seaman were the carpenters. The master mason was John Sanford, assisted by his two brothers. Mathew Hall, the father of George Hall, the first mayor of the City of Brooklyn, was the painter.

The foundation stones for the third and last church to be built on the site were the stones from the walls of the earlier church. The stones for the walls of the new church were quarried at Hurlgate and brought by water to Gowanus and Dentons Mill by Jeremiah Van Dyke. In order to save money, volunteers from the congregation hauled the stones to Flatbush from the Brooklyn ports. The brown stone that forms the lower part of the building was taken from the Brooklyn woods. The brick around the doors and windows, which Strong thought "the only matter of bad taste in the building," came from Holland as ballast in one of the ships belonging to the Honorable John Vanderbilt.

The Church bell was a gift from John Vanderbilt and was almost lost. According to Reverend Strong:

> The vessel in which this bell was shipped, was captured by the British, on her passage to this country, and carried into Halifax, and from the fact that the bell had on it this inscription, "Presented to the Reformed Dutch Church of Flatbush, by John Vanderbilt," it was presumed that both vessel and cargo, belonged to a Holland merchant, and she was on the point of being condemned, when Mr. Charles Clarkson, the son-in-law of Mr. Vanderbilt, went to Halifax and testified that he [Vanderbilt] was a citizen of the United States.

The happy part of the ending is that the bell did arrive. Unhappily, the second or third time it was rung was to mark the death of John Vanderbilt, who died in November 1796 at the age of fifty-seven. It was said of him:

> He was a merchant of distinguished probity—a real patriot—and affectionate relative—a sincere friend, and a worthy man. Blessed with affluence, he displayed a spirit of munificence in promoting the interest of his country, of religion and virtue. The moderation and conciliatory disposition which accompanied and conducted his virtues, secured him through life, an esteem almost unrivalled, and rendered his death, a great loss to the public, and to his family irreparable.

The church that has been in continuous use and still has an active congregation was completed on December 6, 1796. It cost £4,873.7.7 exclusive of cartage that was performed by members of the congregation. The church had ninety-seven pews plus those reserved for the elders and deacons, the pastor, and the justice of the peace. The pews were sold at public auction that raised £2,013.7.9. At its dedication in January, 1797, the Reverend Martinus Schoonmaker preached the morning service in Dutch and the Reverend Peter Lowe conducted the afternoon service in English.

THE SCHOOL

In keeping with the strong community values of religion and education, beginning in 1659 when Adrian Hegeman became the first schoolmaster and continuing until 1802 when the Erasmus Academy was opened as a secular academy, there was a school affiliated with the church. Until 1762 the classes were taught in Dutch.

School was in session five days a week from September to June. In addition to the secular curriculum of reading, writing, and figures, there was also a set course of religious instruction. The school bell was rung at 8:00 a.m. to announce the beginning of the school day, which began with a student reading the Morning Prayer. At 11:00 a.m., before recessing for dinner another prayer was recited. The afternoon session began at 1:00 p.m. with a prayer and at 4:00 p.m., with the close of the school day, the final prayer was recited.

The schoolmaster was hired on behalf of the community by the town magistrates. An agreement made in 1681 with Johannes Van Eckkellen, spelling out his religious and secular duties, was typical.

> Johannes Van Eckkellen, a young man from New Albany, is hereby called and accepted, on the first day of October 1681, with the advice and consent of the Honorable Magistrates, to perform the duties heretofore required of Jan Thibaud [the former schoolmaster], in manner following: (1.) He shall serve the Church and School, according to the existing ordinances, in the same manner, as they have been heretofore performed by the above named Jan Thibaud, and as hereunder written,—(2.) this contract shall take effect, from the fist day of October, Inst. and continue to the first day of May next, for the purpose of making a trial of each other in the mean time.—(3.) For the performance above duties he shall be entitled to receive the sum of 234 guilders, in grain, valued in Seewant, the other privileges appertaining to the calling, during the time specified.

The terms were apparently agreeable to both parties because Eckkellen served in that post until 1700. Although valued by the community, the position of schoolmaster was low-paying and in order to support themselves and their families, the schoolmasters also served the church. Among his church duties the schoolmaster was required to:

> . . . keep the church clean, and ring the bell three times before the people assemble to attend the preaching and catechising. Also before the sermon is commenced, he shall read a chapter out of the Holy Scriptures, and that, between the second and third ringing of the bell. After the third ringing he shall read the ten-commandments, and the twelve articles of our faith, and then take the lead in the singing. In the afternoon after the third ringing of the bell, he shall read a short chapter, or one of the Psalms of David, as the congregation are assembling: and before divine service commences, shall introduce it, by the singing of a Psalm or Hymn.

The first person to teach in the English language was Petrus Van Steenburgh, who was the schoolmaster from 1762 to 1773. It was said that Mr. Steenburgh was very strict about speaking English and that he had devised a novel way to punish students who spoke Dutch during the school day. The method, according to Reverend Strong's description, appears to be a variation on the game of "hot potato" or "musical chairs:"

> In order to detect these persons, [Steenburgh] had a pewter token about the size of a dollar, which was given to the [student] who first spoke a Dutch word

> after the school was opened. [That student] gave it to the next one whom he heard speak Dutch, and so it passed from one to another; but the boy in whose possession the token was found at the close of the school day appears to have been the scapegoat for the whole, for he was severely ferruled upon the hand by the faithful Petrus Van Steenburgh, who took great delight in finding the successful operation of his most ingenious device. . . .

The school remained church-affiliated until the Erasmus Academy was founded as a secular institution shortly after the American Revolution. The new academy symbolized their new status as Americans and marked the beginning of the revitalization of Flatbush after the devastation of the British occupation.

Dutch Rule

At first, because of its sparse population, western Long Island was governed by a governor general, an appointee of the Dutch West India Company who was based in New Amsterdam. The affairs of Flatbush until 1653 were administered by the Schout (sheriff-judge), an appointee of the governor general. This manner of governing was unsatisfactory as it quickly became corrupt and arbitrary. In Holland, towns were largely autonomous and their inhabitants were accustomed to a voice in town affairs. In 1653 at a convention of the Dutch towns, representatives demanded a political system resembling that of Holland. Governor Stuyvesant was outraged; however, he did increase municipal privileges and finally agreed to allow the towns their council of schepens (aldermen or magistrates). The town of Flatbush was permitted three schepens who were appointed by the governor general from dual lists (lists that submitted two names for each position). The schepens were empowered to conduct the town's affairs but were subordinate to the *schout-fiscal*, also an appointee of the governor general. Unlike the English towns, there were no elections or town meetings. Residents could petition for redress of their grievances. In secular matters authority resided in the councils and the governor general. In religious matters that power belonged to the Classis of Amsterdam, the central body of the Reformed Dutch Church.

By contrast, their English counterparts insisted on the political rights they were entitled to as Englishmen. Beginning with the Mayflower Compact in 1620, they achieved some form of elected representation and a measure of local self-determination. The set of political rights that were embedded in the English culture did not resonate as strongly with the Dutch.

The Dutch world-view was commercial and they were content with the level of material well-being they had achieved. The farmers of Flatbush were focused on their farms, their homes, their social community, and their church. This complacency, which the conquering English agreed not to disturb, allowed the British to capture New Netherlands in 1664 without firing a shot. Later, on the eve of the Battle of Brooklyn, at the start of the American Revolution, it was one of the reasons that the patriots mistrusted them. Whether deserved or not, the poor opinion of many American patriots toward the Dutch farmers of Kings County was summed up by Captain Alexander

Graydon, an American officer held prisoner by the British in Flatbush, who wrote: "[The Dutch] were a people who seemed thoroughly disposed to submit to any power that might be imposed on them."

English Rule

After conquering New Netherlands in 1664, the first action the English took was to change the name of the colony to New York. Second, they changed town governance by installing a system of eight overseers, later called commissioners, who were elected by the free holders of the town for two-year terms. Third, in 1683, for administrative purposes, the English consolidated the six towns into Kings County. In 1684 they replaced the Dutch land patents without disturbing the underlying ownership of the land. Changes took place gradually and naturally. Slowly, without trauma, the English language began to replace Dutch, indicative of a normal transition from the strongly Dutch culture to a hybrid English-Dutch culture that was taking place.

Much credit for this seamless change should go to Colonel Richard Nicolls, the British conqueror of New Netherlands and first English governor of New York (1664–1668). Immediately upon taking up his duties he put into place a policy of firmness with tolerance, and was more liberal in the governance of the Dutch than he was in the governance of the English. Under his policies the Dutch were permitted to retain their personal freedoms, including the laws governing inheritance that were more liberal to women than English law. They were also allowed their local autonomy, their language, and their close ties to the Netherlands, including their religious ties to the Reformed Dutch Church. To settle disputes, a system of arbitration in which the disputants could select their arbitrators was established. This system of resolving disputes was traditional. Nicolls also ordered his troops to treat the Dutch inhabitants with "charity and brotherhood." Officers who did not accord respect to the people of New Netherlands were cashiered. His successor, Governor Francis Lovelace (1668–1673) continued these favorable policies that were formalized under terms of the final Dutch surrender in 1674. Thus the day-to-day lives of the people were hardly affected. The exception to the leniency of English rule was in the treatment of slaves.

Under English authority the laws governing slaves were harsh and restrictive. Although from the 1640s forward slaves were in great demand under Dutch rule and Flatbush had been one of the major slave-holding areas in the north, slavery had never been institutionalized under law and subjected to legal strictures. Slaves were treated more as indentured servants and could move freely through society. Since most families had only a few slaves each, they generally lived in the attic or lofts of the farm houses. Under a policy of "half-freedom"—a practice alien to the English—slaves were permitted to work for themselves on condition that they provided a certain amount of free labor or product to their owners.

Dutch attitudes toward slavery allowed African Americans, both slave and free, greater participation in the community than enslaved or free blacks under English law. Under the Dutch slaves were permitted to own land. They were also allowed to learn to read and write. They could testify for and against both African Americans and whites in courts of law. Furthermore, slaves could be members of the militia and in time of trouble they were counted on to aid in defense. Historian David Kobrin sums up the difference by quoting the perplexed remarks of an English traveler regarding the treatment of slaves in New Netherlands: "[T]heir blacks were very free and familiar; sometimes sauntering about among the whites at meal time, with hat on head, and freely joining occasionally in conversations."

Similarly, in his book *In the Matter Of Color* (1978) jurist and historian A. Leon Higginbotham Jr. quotes the description of slavery under the Dutch, published in 1883, by George W. Williams, one of the earliest black historians:

> [African Americans] went and came among their class without let or hindrance. They were married and given in marriage; they sowed, and in many instances, gathered an equitable share of the fruits of their labors. If there were no schools for them, there were no laws against an honest attempt to acquire knowledge at seasonable times . . . [The Dutch] could not habilitate slavery with all the hideous features it wore in Virginia and Massachuetts. The slaves could not escape the good influences of the mild government of the New Netherlands, nor could the Hollanders without the brightness and goodness of their hearts from their domestic slaves.

Unlike the Dutch, English law defined the African-American slave as chattel, prevented slave marriages, limited slave mobility, forbade teaching slaves to read, and did not accept slave testimony in courts of law against whites. In New Netherlands, slaves, until 1682, continued to hold on to their Dutch status that considered them akin to indentured servants, "as servants for life." In that year New York began to redefine slavery in conformance with the law of the other English colonies. In 1702, the "Act for Regulating Slaves" formalized the chattel status of slaves. This law created problems for Flatbush, one of the largest slave-owning areas in the north. In 1698, of the 476 people living in Flatbush seventy-one, or 15 percent of the population, were slaves. In 1746 the town's population increased to a total of 540 people; 25 percent of whom or 134 persons were slaves. By 1820 the population increased to 1,041 persons and 211, or 20 percent, were slaves, along with eighty-three free African Americans. In 1827 New York outlawed slavery.

Chapter Two

FLATBUSH AND THE AMERICAN REVOLUTION

"With the first shots fired at Brooklyn—the bloodiest clash of the American Revolution—the age of 'democratic warfare' had begun . . ."

—John J. Gallagher
The Battle of Brooklyn 1776

Even before the Declaration of Independence was signed, both the Americans and British knew that war was inevitable. They also recognized the strategic importance of New York City. The city, situated at the southern tip of Manhattan Island on the great harbor, was the commercial center of the colonies and their most important port and transportation hub with many inland trade routes radiating from it. At the start of the war New York and Long Island were in American hands, although both places had large populations of Tory (British) sympathizers.

In order to supervise the city's defenses, Washington began setting up his New York headquarters in March 1776, several months before the Declaration of Independence was signed. He was acutely aware that if the British gained control of New York, they could, in his words, "stop the intercourse between the northern and southern Colonies, upon which depends the Safety of America." His fellow patriot John Adams of Massachusetts called New York "a kind of key to the whole continent."

For the British, capturing New York satisfied two important objectives. First, they wanted to physically divide the country and isolate the two centers of revolutionary activity, Virginia and New England, from each other. Second, as the great naval power they were, they needed the harbor to maintain their supply lines. In order to control the harbor they had to have control of Long Island, particularly Brooklyn Heights, the high ground directly across from Manhattan that overlooked it.

The situation in the three counties (Nassau County did not yet exist) of Long Island was complicated. Suffolk County, on the eastern end of the island, was the largest. It had originally been settled by migrants from New England who had maintained strong cultural, political, and economic ties to the area that was at the center of revolutionary activity. It shared the New Englanders' values and strongly supported the patriot cause. The most conservative county was Queens, at the center of the island. Most of its English and Dutch population remained loyal to the crown. The exception was the town of North Hempstead that had close ties to Connecticut, just across Long Island Sound. Kings County (Brooklyn), on the island's western end, was the most ambivalent. Its location made it strategically important to both the British and the Americans.

Of the six original towns in Kings County, five had been settled by the Dutch and one, Gravesend, had been settled by religious English dissidents under a Dutch land patent. Even though the English had ruled the area for more than one hundred years, the Dutch had been allowed to maintain their social order and culture. The English had not upset their property arrangements, nor had they interfered with their ties to Holland. Even the language was allowed to evolve slowly and naturally from Dutch to English. Thus the general prosperity of Kings County's towns had continued uninterrupted and the residents, satisfied with their material well-being, never adopted the political culture of the English colonies nor their demands for autonomy. Although history has often characterized Kings County as loyalists, its population was clearly divided among loyalists, patriots, and neutrals—the latter hard-working, apolitical farmers who hoped against hope that the war would "go away."

The depth of ambivalence in Kings County was reflected in the preaching of its two Flatbush ministers: the Reverend Ulpianus Van Sinderen, who had assumed his ministerial duties at the First Dutch Reform Church in 1746; and the Reverend Johannes Casparus Rubel, who took up his duties as co-minister in 1759. At the start of the American Revolution, these two ministers held opposite points of view, which were reflected in the cold relationship between them. It is said Reverend Van Sinderen so detested Reverend Rubel that he went out of his way to avoid meeting him. The conflict between the two ministers was paralleled in the congregation. The supporters of the Revolution came to church only when Reverend Van Sinderen preached and those who favored the British attended services only when Reverend Rubel was on the pulpit.

The Reverend Van Sinderen was described as "a lean and shriveled little man with a triangular sharp-pointed hat, and silver flowing locks . . ." who always seemed to be in a hurry, frenetically rushing from place to place. Perhaps tongue in cheek the historian Henry R. Stiles commented on Van Sinderen's long windedness by noting that he was "distinguished by a species of pulpit eloquence which might be truly said to 'bring matters home to men's business and bosoms.' " Reverend Strong considered Van Sinderen learned but sometimes lacking in judgment. He tells this story:

> He [Van Sinderen] was too much in the habit of introducing the occurrences of the week previous in his sermons, on the Sabbath, and often would allude to very trifling circumstances. . . . On one occasion, a good old Elder, who had borne with the Dominie in this particular, till his patience was exhausted, very injudiciously, under the excitement of his feelings, rose in his seat during divine service, and interrupted Mr. Van Sineren, by saying, they had called him to preach the gospel, and not to detail to them such matters. The Dominie, indignant at being stopped in his discourse leaned over the pulpit, and replied, "You, Philip Nagle, if you can preach the gospel better than I can, come up here and try."

His eccentricities notwithstanding, Van Sinderen was a principled leader and a staunch patriot who was unwavering in his support of the American cause. An illustration of Van Sinderan's courage is the story of how, speaking in the Dutch language, he led his Flatbush congregation in prayers for an American victory while British officers sat, unaware, in the church. His counterpart, Reverend Rubel, preached the opposite. In a sermon delivered in Flatbush on the text "honor the king," Rubel said among other things, "people could do as well without a head as without a king." Many worshippers were deeply offended.

In his book *History of Flatbush*, Reverend Strong tells this story:

> On the first or second evening of their arrival in Flatbush, a drunken revel took place among the British. In rifling the houses, the were directed by John Rubel, to a quantity of wine, which had been left in the house of Mr. David Clarkson . . . Mr. Clarkson was a strong whig [patriot] and after they had vented their spite at him, and his principles, by destroying his furniture, and abusing his premises in a shameful manner, their attention was called, under the direction of their guide, to his wines. These, the greater part of which were specially imported and were very choice, Mr. Clarkson had bottled and stored away in an upper apartment, in the wing of his house, and had built up a partition to conceal them. Rubel had seen this, and was well acquainted with the store thus concealed, and being friendly to the British cause, he gave them information of the fact, and actually guided and assisted them on the occasion.

The Reverend Strong, commenting on the debauchery following the discovery of the wines, regretted that the Americans were unaware of the party. Otherwise, he speculated, "a very serious check might have been put on the British advance, if not their whole plan, subverted."

In 1783 the occupation of Long Island ended and the British departed Flatbush. Shortly thereafter, in June 1784, Reverend Van Sinden retired. The congregation declared him Emeritus and he was given a small stipend for life from the church. He died in Flatlands in July 1796.

On the other hand, in 1784 Reverend Rubel faced the Particular Synod, called to investigate complaints of the Flatbush congregation against him. Many witnesses testified to his treasonous behavior toward the American cause and his scandalous activities in his private life. One witness recalled hearing Rubel call patriots "Satan's soldiers." Another said Rubel told him "that all those who opposed the king were accursed, and many were already in hell, and the rest who were not dead would get there." Other witnesses told of Rubel's drunken behavior and wife-beating. One who was visiting Rubel's house saw him strike his wife with his fist. Another man, Gabriel Ellison, testified that Rubel beat his wife so severely that feeling sorry for Mrs. Rubel, he and his wife had taken her in. To get even, Rubel denounced Mr. Ellison from the pulpit. For his behavior Rubel was censured for life and removed from the ministry. He died in 1799 and was interred in the public cemetery of the Dutch Reform Church of Flatbush. He had been the only minister in the long history of the church that was so disgraced.

Preparing for Battle: The British

In June 1776 the British began to assemble their troops in anticipation of a battle for New York. General Sir William Howe (1729–1814), who with his older brother Admiral Lord Richard Howe (1726–1799) would command the British forces in New York, arrived off Staten Island with a fleet of 130 ships and over 9,000 troops on June 25. His brother joined him on July 12 with 150 more ships, including six ships of the line, thirty frigates, and many transports. There were also 13,000 additional soldiers. By the week preceding the Battle of Brooklyn, the British ground forces numbered 32,000 strong, including 10,000 Hessians. In addition, there was a naval force of 10,000 sailors and a contingent of 2,000 Royal Marines, manning thirty warships and over 400 transports. This was the largest assemblage of ships and men ever amassed until World War II. The legendary Spanish Armada had consisted of only 129 ships, less than half the number anchored off the coast of Staten Island. Observers viewing the fleet at anchor described it as a "forest of masts." An American soldier wrote, "I spied as I peeped out the Bay something resembling a wood of pine trees trimmed . . . In about ten minutes the whole Bay was full of shipping as ever it could be. . . . I thought all of London was afloat."

The Howe brothers were confident of a victory. They were sure that their superbly trained and well-armed forces could easily conquer the rebels who were fewer in number and more poorly armed and trained. Nevertheless they were determined to have sufficient troop strength to overwhelm them—and perhaps, they thought, by their show of power intimidate and even discourage them from fighting. After sustaining heavy losses and having 7,000 troops under siege at Boston, the British were determined not to repeat the experience in New York.

Prior to the start of hostilities on July 14, in what was essentially a futile gesture, Admiral Howe, in keeping with his very narrowly drawn commission to try to negotiate a last-minute peace, sent a letter to George Washington to see if war could be avoided and British rule reestablished. The letter was addressed to George Washington, Esquire. Washington took umbrage that Admiral Howe had failed to acknowledge his military rank as leader of the American army and address him as General George Washington. He promptly returned the letter unopened. A few days later the admiral again sent a letter addressed George Washington, &c. &c. to be delivered by his envoy, Colonel Paterson. Although polite to Colonel Paterson, who argued that the et ceteras implied everything, Washington, for the second time, refused to take delivery, responding, "it is no less true that they imply anything." Commenting on Washington's rejoinder, Strong wrote: "A noble answer to this repeated insult to himself and his country, and a clear presage of the practical wisdom, courage and firmness of him to whom America, under God, had committed her cause."

This was the last official contact the Americans and British would have until they met on the battlefield on August 27, 1776.

Preparing for Battle: The Americans

On paper Washington had about 19,000 men for the defense of New York. However, in reality, only about 10,000 were available for duty. These troops varied in their abilities and preparations for war. On one hand, there were the excellently trained and uniformed contingents of Colonel John Haslet's Delaware Continentals and Colonel William Smallwood's First Maryland Regiment—the Maryland 400. These men fought under the command of General William Alexander, who preferred to be called by his Scottish title, Lord Stirling. Although badly outnumbered, the Delaware and Maryland troops fought so fiercely and so heroically that they made it possible for Washington and his army to avoid capture. A distressed Washington, helpless to send in more aid, watched the fighting from high ground (what is now the corner of Atlantic Avenue and Court Street in Cobble Hill) and cried out, "Good God! What brave fellows I must lose this day." In their book *Gotham* (1999), historians Edwin G. Burrows and Mike Wallace say that by the end of the final Brooklyn battle at the Vechte-Cortelyou, or Old Stone House in Gowanus, only nine of the Marylanders returned; the others were either captured or killed and Lord Stirling was taken prisoner. Other accounts say that of the original Maryland 400 who had come to fight, ninety-six returned and only thirty-five were still able bodied. Without the bravery of these men it is likely that the war would have ended that day with the defeat of the Americans.

On the other hand there were rag-tag bands of poorly trained and armed men, some without uniforms or guns. Although most fought bravely, some deserted. Those who did not leave stayed because Washington had given orders to shoot to kill any man who tried to flee. These men often had little skill and less discipline. For example, military historian John Gallagher in *The Battle of Brooklyn, 1776*, writing about the New York militia that he thought was one of the most inexperienced and poorly equipped, characterized its organizational structure as "primitive," adding that "in many cases [it] was not distinguishable from a band of Neanderthal hunters."

With Admiral Howe's fleet anchored in the Narrows and General Howe occupying Staten Island where his troops had been warmly welcomed, the Americans established a watch along the perimeter of western Long Island to observe ship movements and to warn of invasion. The signal would be fire at night and smoke by day. Intelligence on British movements was essential since almost until the day of battle the Americans had been kept off-balance and were unsure of how or where the British would attack. As a result Washington had to plan for several contingencies, including holding back troops in order to protect Manhattan against an invasion by water.

The second equally important duty of the watch was to prevent the large loyalist population on Long Island from communicating with the fleet or otherwise trafficking with the enemy. When loyalist boats were found the patriots would confiscate their oars and sails, and occasionally dismantle the entire craft. Nevertheless, many communications got through and General Howe was well apprised of American movements.

The Americans were also concerned with the large herds of farm animals and great stores of food in the successful agricultural communities. For them it was imperative that animals and provisions not fall into British hands. Farmers were ordered to drive their animals inland to the Hempstead plain and to put all excess stores—food not immediately needed to feed families—into the fields where it was burnt. Some historians argue that the burning was a punishment to farmers who had been indifferent to the cause. In a letter written to his wife, Captain Josiah Hodgkins of Massachusetts wrote about the unpleasant reception the troops received from the farmers: "Our people are not allowed to tread on the ground scarcely," he complained. "They are not allowed to get orsters [oysters] out of the Cove, and the man forbid them catching eales . . ."

By mid-summer farmers and their families were fleeing Kings County en masse, and those few farmers who did stay to tend their crops sent their families and possessions either further east on the island or to New Jersey. Strong, who later in life knew some of the people and took the most compassionate view of the plight of those farmers, rationalized their behavior:

> We who have been so long accustomed to the sweets of peace know but little of the consternation occasioned by an approaching invading army. The inhabitants had reason to apprehend that should they remain at home they would be cruelly treated, and perhaps massacred. They were regarded as rebels, to whom little quarter would be shown. Hence as expeditiously as possible after the landing of the British troops, the inhabitants of the village either sent or carried off the females and children . . . It was a scene of great confusion and no ordinary distress. Compelled to leave their homes and the greater part of their property, and not knowing what might befall their persons or their families, they committed themselves to the good providence of their God. Some had not gone far before they saw the smoke ascending from the neighborhood of their farms, and knew not that their dwellings were already in flames.

Although the ultimate objective of the British force was Manhattan, strategically, in order to secure their position, they needed to control Brooklyn Heights with its commanding view of the harbor and New York. For the Americans, holding the Heights was crucial. Washington placed General Nathanael Greene, a young officer whom he held in high regard, in charge of the defense. Washington's confidence in Greene was not misplaced. Immediately upon taking up his duties, Greene thoroughly familiarized himself with the terrain. This was important, particularly since some of the British officers, having served in New York, were as familiar (and in some instances more familiar) with the city and its environs as the American patriots. This was particularly true of General Henry Clinton, who devised the successful British battle strategy. Furthermore, although the coastal watch had tried, they were unable to prevent loyalists from communicating with the British. Their intelligence regularly reached the British and kept them fully informed and up-to-date on the activities of the Americans.

For the defense of Brooklyn Heights, Greene established a series of fortifications, including cannon emplacements, along the East River in an interior defensive line running southwest from Wallabout Bay (the present Navy Yard) to Gowanus Creek (today's Gowanus Canal). The approaches to the fortified Heights from the south were protected by troops manning an exterior defensive line about two miles further inland at the four passes in the terminal moraine. The terminal moraine, the most southerly point of the Wisconsin glacier on Long Island, was a rugged spine of glacial rock and rubble that ran west to east from Gowanus to Jamaica and beyond. Also known as the Heights of Guian (Guan) or the Mount Prospect Range, this natural barrier, made almost impassible by thickets and trees, had an elevation of between forty to eighty feet above the flat plain to its south. There were five places where troops could get through, running from west to east.

The first was the shore road, running from Gravesend to Gowanus. This flat road followed the curve of the bay along the western end of Brooklyn and led directly to the main fortifications on the heights. The patriots' strongest fortifications were located here.

The second was the Martense Pass (also known as Martense Lane), the most westerly opening in the terminal moraine that joined the shore road after passing through the area that is now the southern end of Greenwood Cemetery. The Vechte-Cortelyou House, or the Old Stone House as it is known, stood close to the junction of the two roads. On the afternoon of August 27, with the Americans in retreat, the stone house became the scene of the last battle in Brooklyn—a ferocious fight between Lord Stirling's Maryland troops and the British. The Americans sustained enormous casualties—more than 250 died. Their losses, however, were not in vain. The heroic actions of these men bought Washington the time he needed to evacuate his army—thus saving the Revolution.

About a mile and a half east was the Flatbush Pass, the third point, located near what is now the Prospect Park zoo. That day it too was the scene of heavy fighting. The American troops here and at Bedford Pass were under the command of General John Sullivan. They faced Hessian troops under the command of General Leopold Philip de Heister. Henry R. Stiles in *The History of Brooklyn* described the defenses as:

> first, a sort of crescent-shaped intrenchment [*sic*], just within the village of Flatbush, and lying diagonally across the main street, a little south of Judge Martense's house, with a ditch of considerable depth on its northerly side; secondly, a small redoubt, mounting a few pieces of artillery at the "Valley Grove" to guard the passage through the "Porte Road" [a lane diverging from the Flatbush turnpike, and extending to the East River] to Brooklyn.

Near the redoubt was the huge white oak tree that marked the boundary between Flatbush and Brooklyn. It was felled across the road as part of the American defense.

The fourth was Bedford Pass, now the intersection of Bedford and Rodgers Avenues. At that point it was the intersection of the Old Clove Road with the Flatbush and Brooklyn boundary line, and was about a mile to the east of the Flatbush Pass.

Three miles farther east was the Jamaica Pass, the fifth point, which was located along what was then and still is a major road still known as Kings Highway. The pass was at a place near Evergreen Cemetery where the new settlement of New Lots, then still part of the town of Flatbush, was just taking root. Catching the Americans unaware, the British used this pass as their main conduit to circle behind the American lines. Colonel Samuel Miles, who with his men was posted along a ridge between the Bedford Pass and the Jamaica Pass, did not defend this pass. It was through this virtually unguarded opening, furthest from the landing point, that the main body of British soldiers, under the command of General Clinton and Lords Cornwallis and Percy, outflanked the Americans.

Unfortunately for the Americans, just days before the British began their invasion on August 22, General Greene became seriously ill with camp (typhus) fever and had to be replaced. Greene's command was transferred to General Sullivan of New Hampshire, an officer who did not have Washington's full confidence. Evaluating Sullivan, Washington is quoted by military historian John Gallagher as saying, "[Sullivan] has his wants, and he has his foibles . . . a little tincture of vanity and . . . over-desire of being popular, which now and then leads him into some embarrassments."

On August 24, shortly after Sullivan assumed command, Washington made an inspection tour of the lines on Long Island and to his dismay found everything at "loose ends." Henry R. Stiles scribed the total disorder: "Detachments skirmished with the enemy's vanguard, or picked off his sentries, without any orders and with little method—others were little better than marauding parties, who burned the houses of friend and foe alike, and robbed dwellings, barns and hen-roosts with impunity."

The behavior of the troops, according to Stiles, is what angered Washington the most. "Shameful it is," he quotes Washington as saying, "to find that those men who have come hither in defence [*sic*] of the rights of man kind to turn invaders of them, by destroying the substance of their friends. . . . The distinction between a well-regulated army and a mob, is the good discipline and order of the former, and the licentious and disorderly behavior of the latter."

It was after viewing this scene just days before a battle that Washington decided it was necessary to bring in another general in order to establish discipline among the troops. He settled on General Israel Putnam of Connecticut, who wanted the post. Putnam, an experienced general, took up his command on August 25, two days before the Battle of Brooklyn began. Washington's orders to Putnam included the charge that he "form a proper line of defence [*sic*] around [his] encampment and works, on the most advantageous grounds," and that "[T]he woods should be secured by abates, etc., where necessary, to make the enemy's approach as difficult as possible."

Putnam was not familiar with the terrain upon which the coming battle would be fought, and there is no evidence he made any effort to familiarize himself with it. He took charge of the defense of Brooklyn Heights and Sullivan, his second in command, was charged with holding the center of the line at the Flatbush and Bedford Passes along the Heights of Guian. General Alexander (Lord Stirling), who was also deployed to Brooklyn on August 25 and was subordinate to Putnam, commanded the Maryland and Delaware troops assigned to guard the western end at the Shore Road and Martense Pass. The Americans expected that the brunt of the British attack would be against those positions.

According to Burrows and Wallace, Putnam "was a capable veteran of the French and Indian War who had faced Howe at Bunker Hill. 'Don't fire until you see the whites of their eyes' he is supposed to have said. 'Then fire low'." Gallagher, however, points out that the harassing techniques Putnam had employed so effectively during the French and Indian War failed against the well-trained professional army he now faced. Washington admonished Putnam for the pointless forays that the Americans were making to harass the British. He considered the actions wasteful. "[A] kind of fire which tended to disgrace our men as soldiers and rend our defence [*sic*] contemptible in the eyes of the enemy," he said.

By bringing in an experienced general, particularly one with the stature of Putnam, Washington had hoped to strengthen his position and mount a solid defense. However, assigning Putnam seems to have had the opposite effect. Gallagher, for instance, acknowledged that Putnam was charismatic and stories of his exploits in the earlier French and Indian war gave him a larger-than-life persona. Nevertheless, Gallagher views Putnam's abilities with disdain. To make his point, he cites witness accounts of Putnam behaving erratically and quotes descriptions of the disheveled general rushing about on horseback giving almost purposeless orders.

In more stinging criticisms, Gallagher faults Putnam for ignorance of the field of battle and for having an incoherent battle plan due to his lack of knowledge of military tactics. As an example of Putnam's incompetence, Gallagher points out that both Generals Greene and Sullivan had maintained nightly patrols along the Brooklyn roads. Under General Putnam these patrols were stopped. Furthermore, Gallagher views Putnam's decision to remain behind the lines and never tour the ground where the battle would be fought as disastrous.

Stiles is even more severe in his criticisms, accusing Putnam of not obeying direct orders and of dereliction of duty by leaving Jamaica Pass unguarded in spite of the nearby presence of the enemy. Stiles, relying on the expert analysis of military historian Henry B. Dawson, Esquire, adopts Dawson's conclusions:

> From these facts it appears conclusively that General Putnam paid no attention to the orders of General Washington, respecting the security of the passes, and the advice of General Sullivan on the same subject, was also disregarded, his patrols withdrawn, and the command outside the lines, where his knowledge of the ground rendered him peculiarly useful, taken from him and given to another; that with the enemy encamped in full force within a few miles of his position, he quietly remained at Brooklyn, without reconnoitering that enemy's position, or sending out a scout; that he withdrew guards and failed to remount them, where they were essential to his safety; and finally that his ignorant, self-conceited inefficiency, the enemy is indebted for one of the greatest victories of the war, and his country for one of the most disastrous defeats, both military and moral, which it ever had experienced.

However, other writers seem to differ, and place more of the blame for the disaster on General Sullivan. Strong, who was writing closest to the event and knew witnesses and participants, seems to blame the laxity of the American defenses on Colonel Miles of Pennsylvania, who was in charge of the left wing (eastern end) at Jamaica Pass for not perceiving the approach of the enemy, and General Sullivan who failed to discover why one of his horseback patrols had not returned. Strong puts the onus for the failures of that day onto General Sullivan:

> General Sullivan neglected to send out fresh scouts, probably expecting that the English would direct their principal efforts against the right wing, under Lord Stirling. . . . Thus he suffered the American army to be surprised, and almost before the battle commenced, the fate of the day determined.

In *The Battle for New York*, Barnet Schecter writes that Colonel Miles had discovered the British troop movements, and tried to warn Sullivan that the British were going to come through Jamaica Pass. He quotes Miles:

> On the landing of the British army on Long Island, I was ordered over with my rifle regiment to watch their motions. I marched near to the village of Flatbush where the Highlanders then lay, but they moved the next day to Gen'l Howe's camp, and their place was supplied by the Hessians. I lay here within cannon shot of the Hessian camp for four days without receiving a single order from Gen'l Sullivan. . . . The day before the action he came to the camp, and I then told him the situation of the British army; that Gen'l Howe, with the main body, lay on my left, about a half or two miles, and I was convinced when the army moved that Gen'l Howe would fall into the Jamaica Road, and I hoped there were troops there to watch them. Notwithstanding this information, which indeed he might have obtained from his own observation, if he had attended to his duty as a general ought to have done, no steps were taken, but there was a small redoubt in front of the village that seemed to take up the whole of his attention.

The Invasion of Flatbush

On August 22, under cover provided by the guns of the *Rainbow* and other men-of-war, 4,000 light infantry with forty cannons were transported in flatboats from Staten Island and without incident landed at Denyse's Ferry (now the foot of the Verrazzano Bridge in Fort Hamilton). Shortly thereafter, under the cover of guns from the frigates *Phoenix*, *Rose*, and *Grayhound*, an additional 15,000 men, also without incident, were landed by rowboat at Bath on Gravesend Bay. Within three hours 19,000 of the world's best-trained troops had come ashore.

Although a contingent of 200 Pennsylvania riflemen, under Colonel Edward Hand, watched the landing from high ground, they offered no resistance. Gallagher quotes a Hessian officer commenting on the ease of the two-stage British landing operation.

"When we disembarked on Staten Island, they might have destroyed a good many of our people with two six-pounders," the officer noted, "and now [on Long Island] they might have made it very nasty for us."

As Hand's men were retreating to Flatbush where they would skirmish with Hessian troops and later fight at the Flatbush Pass, they set fire to nearby wheat fields in order to keep them from falling into enemy hands. According to Strong, they also set fire to the Peter Lefferts house and several other houses as well.

The invading forces, led by Lord Cornwallis, immediately began moving east toward Flatbush and Flatlands. Flatbush became the main staging area for the battle to come. Strong described the encampment at Flatbush: "They encamped in a diagonal direction across the village. Their tents extended from the little lane over the farms of Hendrick Vanderveer, of J.C. Bergen, of Jacobus Vandeventer and so on, in a northeasterly line towards the road leading to New Lots. The main body however, were on the south of the church and west of the main (Flatbush) street."

Over the next few days, the skirmishing between the sides continued, with the British gaining ground. According to Strong's description:

> They soon possessed themselves of the intrenchment which had been thrown up by the Americans, in the north of the village. To defend themselves against an expected attack from the American troops, who, from the woods, kept up a scattered firing, they knocked out large portholes in the house of Adrian Hegeman, which stood on the spot where Mrs. Cynthia Lefferts is now living. This house was built of stone, and the object of making the holes in the wall, was to enable them to fire their cannon at the Americans under cover. The house of Mr. Lefferts Martense, on the opposite side of the road, was also taken possession of, and prepared as a sort of fortification. It was built of wood, fronting south, and having a roof on the north side, which extended to within a few feet of the ground. In this roof they cut many holes, through which they could fire their muskets. Still further to defend themselves, or render their firing upon the Americans more effective, they set fire to the houses which stood between them and the woods, and from behind which, the American riflemen discharged their guns . . . These houses were those of Jeremiah Vanderbilt and Leffert Lefferts, on the west and Evert Hegeman on the east side of the road.

The day after the invasion, August 23, General Howe issued the following proclamation:

> By his EXCELLENCY, THE Hon. WM. HOWE, General and Commander-in-Chief of all His Majesty's forces within the Colonies . . .
>
> Whereas, it is represented that many of the loyal inhabitants of this Island have been compelled by the leaders in rebellion, to take up arms against His Majesty's Government, Notice is hereby given to all persons so forced into

> rebellion, that on delivering themselves up at said quarters of the Army, they will be received as faithful subjects, have permits peaceably to return to their respective dwellings, and meet with full protection for their persons and property. All those who choose to take up arms for the restoration of order and good government within this Island, shall be disposed of in the best manner, and have every encouragement that can be expected.

According to Stiles not many people took Howe up on his offer. However, Stiles speculates that it wasn't because the population was averse to the British. It was just that people did not want to take sides until they could determine the winning side. The next day, August 24, George Washington sent an exhortation to his soldiers:

> The enemy have now landed on Long Island, and the hour is fast approaching in which the honor and success of this army, and the safety of our bleeding country, will depend. Remember, officers and soldiers, that you are freemen, fighting for the blessings of liberty, and slavery will be your portion, if you do not acquit yourselves like men. Remember how your courage and spirit have been despised and traduced by your cruel invaders, though they have found by dear experience at Boston, Charlestown and other places, what a few brave men, contending in their own land, and in the best of causes can do against hirelings and mercenaries. Be cool, but be determined; do not fire at a distance, but wait for orders from your officers. It is the general's express orders, that if any man attempt to skulk, lie down, or retreat without orders, he be instantly shot down as an example. He hopes no such will be found in his army; but on the contrary, that every one for himself resolving to conquer or die, and trusting in the smiles of Heaven upon such just a cause, will behave with bravery and resolution. . . .

But not everyone heeded Washington's words. The American forces were smaller in number, more poorly armed, and with few exceptions lacked discipline. The New York Provincial Congress had only begun to recruit its 3,000-man quota for the Continental Army in late June and was having a difficult time. Earlier the Staten Island militia had joined with the British. As the Americans prepared for the Battle of Brooklyn, very few Kings County men were in their ranks. The Kings County militia had been ordered into service under the command of Lieutenant Colonel Nicholas Cowenhoven of Flatbush and Major Barent Johnson (father of General Jeremiah Johnson) of Bushwick. According to Stiles, many of these men took the first opportunity to change sides and join the British army, while others just hid or went home.

The most prominent of the Kings County deserters was Colonel Nicholas Cowenhoven, a scion of one of Flatbush's earliest and most prominent families. According to Stiles, Cowenhoven left his position and was later seen in Flatbush in the company of British officers. He was soon captured by the Americans and brought to Harlem Heights, where he was imprisoned. However, when it came time for his trial, the witnesses against him could not be found. It was believed that powerful friends of his had spirited them away. Upon returning home to Flatbush, Cowenhoven continued to do business with the British. In 1783 he and others were indicted for treason, and once again he was saved, this time through the intervention of Alexander Hamilton. In an amazing reversal of political fortune, Cowenhoven, shortly after the adoption of the Constitution, was named one of the government commissioners who investigated the claims against the state by persons who had suffered losses by the actions of American troops in 1776. He later was appointed chief judge of the Court of Common Pleas of Kings County. Of Cowenhoven, Stiles remarks, "In view of his evident sympathy with the British cause, we can only regard his loan of money, in 1782 to Major Wyckoff, as merely a politic concession to the rising fortunes of America."

Let the Battle Begin

The face of war changed on the morning of August 27, 1776, when a poorly disciplined, badly outnumbered army faced the world's greatest military power. "The Battle of Brooklyn," wrote military historian John Gallagher:

> was the first general engagement between large, organized armies in the first of all the great "participatory" patriotic wars to come. It was the first time the fledgling Continental Army acted as the agent of an independent nation, one founded on democratic principles. The battle was fought by men with a cause they were willing to die for. They faced an army of professional soldiers more used to fighting other professionals in the familial, territorial and commercial disputes of their employers. . . . The Americans in the New World were in the process of developing new values; the British were defending traditional ones.

On the day that it was first challenged, August 27, 1776, America was less than two months old.

On the evening of August 26, under the cover of darkness, General Sir Henry Clinton, leaving his tents standing and fires burning, began to silently move his men east toward the Jamaica Pass. General Clinton, who was familiar with the area, had proposed the strategy to General Howe, who had reluctantly agreed. It was a dangerous move, but if successful would be devastating to the Americans—and perhaps end the war right then. In order to execute it, the large army had to be secretly moved six miles at night through hostile territory and face many unforeseen dangers, such as hidden traps or ambushes. The line of march was in fact seen by Captain Cornelius Vanderveer, of the Flatbush militia, from his home. He explained, "that although he was near the fence fronting his house, on the road, he could scarcely hear them." Apparently he did not sound an alarm. Some days after the battle Vanderveer, in the dead of night, stole from his house to retrieve his arms and military accoutrements that he had hidden a few days earlier after having lost a skirmish with the British. A British patrol caught him as he was stealing back to his house and arrested him for wearing the uniform and carrying his arms. He was sent off to prison and, according to Strong, almost hanged. However, while awaiting the hangman's noose in a New Utrecht prison he had the good fortune to see Captain Miller, an officer whom he knew. Through the graces of this officer Vanderveer was saved. The price, however, was a "protection" that required a pledge of alligence to the king. Vanderveer accepted the protection on the condition that he not be made to fight against his country. Throughout the siege, Vanderveer is said to have provided material aid and money to the American cause.

The country roads were not empty at night. Farmers carrying their produce to market and people coming home from local taverns were among those who traveled late. Anticipating such civilian encounters, British troops were ordered to arrest the travelers and hold them until after the fighting. Because of the great danger to them of being spotted, the British allowed themselves twelve hours to travel the five miles to Jamaica Pass and then an additional three miles back to Bedford Village. Several local guides aided them. Strong seems to have known their identity, but declined to divulge it, saying that the men were forced under duress. Nevertheless, he comments: "This may be true, but their agency on this occasion was most disastrous to the American cause." Both Stiles and Gallagher believe the guides were Tories (British sympathizers). Along their route there were two known bottlenecks, one at Schoonmaacher's (Shoemaker's) Bridge that crossed Goose Creek into New Lots, and the other at Jamaica Pass. The narrowness of these spots would have allowed relatively few men to pinion the attacking army long enough for reinforcements to be sent. The British approached both these places very cautiously, although they had received intelligence that neither was guarded.

After crossing the bridge without incident, the last obstacle before them was the Jamaica Pass, a narrow passage that in spite of intelligence to the contrary Howe believed had to be guarded. Just before the pass, the army arrived at a small settlement near a public house that stood at what today would be the intersection of Broadway and Jamaica Avenue. The primary source for the events that took place there, relied on by both Stiles and Gallagher, is a narrative by William Howard Jr., who was present on the night in question and with his father helped guide the British forces. In their narratives, however, Gallagher refers to this inn as the Rising Sun Tavern and Stiles as Howard's Halfway House.

According to the story, with their troops surrounding the houses to prevent an alarm from being raised, General Howe (disguised as a civilian), General Clinton, and two aids entered the tavern and asked for something to drink. Howe began a conversation with the tavern owner William Howard. He told Howard that he needed somebody to guide him around the Jamaica Pass, and Howard, who had recognized the general, replied, "we belong to the other side," and on principle declined to give the general any help. General Howe responded, saying, "That's alright—stick to your country or stick to your principles, but, Howard, you are my prisoner, and must guide my men over the hill."

When Howard tried to refuse again, General Howe warned him that "if he refused, he would have him shot through the head." The Howards, having no choice, led Howe around the pass using the Rockaway path that went through what is now Evergreen Cemetery. Howard Jr.'s narrative, as quoted by Gallagher, continued:

> Lord Howe inquired minutely about the road through the hills, and the position of the hills, the position of the American guard, supposed by him to be occupying that place. So assured was he of the presence there of a strong force, it appearing so incredible that so favorable a position for resisting his passage should not be occupied, that he did not take the precaution of sending out his scouts to ascertain the fact. My father, thus compelled to serve the cause of the enemy was marched out under a guard, who had orders to shoot him if he attempted to desert, and I was taken along with him.

Howard recalled that at the time of the march the moon had already set, and the men moved in total darkness. Behind the guides came people Howard called "the pioneers." Their job was to saw down any tree in the path that might block the cannons. The British did not use axes because they feared the noise would alarm the Americans, whom Howe was so sure were guarding the pass. "This force [of Americans]" Howard continued, "was supposed to be stationed in the hills about a quarter of a mile from the tavern near where the Toll House on the Brooklyn and Jamaica turnpike stands." Although as Howard Jr. remarked, Howe's Tory guides had given him excellent intelligence concerning the light guard at the pass, Howe was shocked to find it so.

The fighting began shortly after midnight on August 27 when a detachment of English soldiers under Major General James Grant engaged the American left flank that was guarding the Shore (Gowanus) Road and Martense Pass. It was defended by American troops commanded by General William Alexander (Lord Stirling). At about the same time, at the center of the line, approximately 800 Hessians under the command of General Leopold Philip de Heister engaged with the American troops commanded by General Sullivan at the Battle (Flatbush) Pass near the Port or Valley Road. The Americans believed that these engagements signaled the main thrust of the British attack. In the ensuing fight, neither side appeared to be victorious. However, unrealized by the Americans, the fighting on the part of the British was diversionary. It was designed to distract in order to allow their main force, 14,000 strong and led by General Howe and commanded by General Clinton and Lords Percy and Cornwallis, to circle behind the Americans from the east. Although it was a risky strategy, the maneuver, known as "turning the enemy's flank," was a great success. According to Stiles:

> When the British column reached "Bedford Corners," the profound silence and secrecy which had previously characterized their movements, gave way to a feeling of exultant joy. They felt assured that the great object of their long and weary night march was fully accomplished; their bands struck up lively strains of martial music, and with elastic step, the troops pressed eagerly forward towards Brooklyn.

This turning point of the battle came at approximately 9:00 a.m. when General Clinton fired his canon, signaling that he was behind the American lines. It was only then, according to Gallagher, that the Americans recognized the British army had left Flatbush. As Gallagher described it, the British line was "extended from [the Flatbush road and Jamaica turnpike] to Bedford, and at the distance of half a mile from the rear of the Americans, who were contesting possession of the Flatbush hills with De Heister—all unconscious that the trap had sprung upon them, and that they were hemmed in on all sides." Stiles added, "Sullivan, indeed seems to have been so completely duped by the feint which Grant was making on his right in the direction of Gowanus, that he quite neglected to send out any fresh patrols towards Jamaica, although he foretold that the real danger would come from this quarter." Fatal mistake! The battle was lost before it had begun.

With Clinton's army behind them, and Grant and the Hessians in front of them, the Americans were trapped and the pursuing army gave them no quarter. During the last stand, the final battle at the Old Stone House near the Porte Road, General Stirling and the Marylanders made a heroic effort to break through the lines of Lord Cornwallis, who had circled in behind them and cut off their retreat to the American side. For twenty-eight minutes Stirling and the Marylanders fought. Although the numbers were overwhelmingly against them, the Americans tried several times to break through the enemy's lines, only to be repulsed. In the end, more than 250 of the Marylanders were lost or captured. Lord Stirling, unwilling to surrender himself to the British, surrendered to the German General de Heister. His actions and the courage of his men, fighting against superior numbers, made it possible for other men to escape to American lines.

By noon the battle was over. Approximately 5,000 men faced an enemy that numbered close to 20,000. According to General Howe's records, the only evidence available, the Americans lost 3,300 men; the British loss was 367. Nevertheless, that night 3,000 men were safe behind American lines. Howe, for tactical reasons, decided to wait for his heavy munitions to reach his camp before attacking.

Bad weather on August 28 gave the Americans a chance to regroup and add reinforcements. It also gave George Washington a chance to visit each of the encampments and encourage his men. The confident British, meanwhile, used the time to build earthworks in preparation for their attack. Their force of about 15,000 men faced the Americans, whose backs were against the water.

Although a thick fog hung over the city for most of the day on August 29, the Americans were able to discover the movements of the British fleet. Some of its ships had traveled up the narrows and were in the harbor. Others had circled around the island and were anchored in Flushing Bay. That afternoon Washington and his generals made the decision to evacuate Long Island. With the British forward positions less than 600 yards in front of them, it was necessary to maintain order and calm among the troops. To prepare the men while maintaining secrecy, the officers were ordered to tell them to get ready for a night attack.

By 10:00 pm the winds had died down and the river was smooth and shrouded in heavy fog. Leaving their campfires burning and their tents standing, the army began boarding rowboats and sailboats manned by a battalion of Marblehead, Massachusetts fishermen and sailors. Washington stood at the stairs of what is now Fulton Ferry, encouraging the men. By 3:00 a.m. the evacuation was complete. Washington rode the last boat to Manhattan. The Americans were alive to fight another day.

There are conflicting views regarding the behavior of the American officers, and larger questions regarding their conduct of the battle. Who was at fault? Were Generals Putnam, Sullivan, or Colonel Miles negligent in their duty? Miles claimed that on or about August 25 he had warned General Sullivan that the elite British troops were being moved east from Flatbush and that they were being replaced at the center of the line by Hessians. From those movements Miles had surmised the attack would come from the east. Events validated that assessment. Having warned General Sullivan, Miles faults him for the debacle. Strong, however, seems to contradict Miles's claim. He states that "Colonel Miles of Pennsylvania, who had charge of the right wing of the American army this night, performed his service with but little exactness, and did not perceive the approach of the enemy."

Gallagher asserts that in the days preceding the battle, General Sullivan was uneasy about his exposed left wing, but lacked manpower to cover it. According to him Sullivan wrote, "I had paid horsemen fifty dollars for patrolling it by night when I had command, as I had no foot for the purpose." Gallagher adds that in the wee hours of August 27, "there were five vedettes a group of officers, not a regular mounted patrol, still on duty the night of the attack. They had been on the alert for five days, however, and were careless that night. They gave some minor resistance but were easily captured." Nevertheless, Stiles and Gallagher fault General Putnam, and to a lesser extent Sullivan, for the disaster.

Flatbush Under Seige

In 1776 Flatbush was a small farming community of approximately 941 people, including slaves. Most were descendants of the original Dutch settlers and even though they lived under English rule for more than one hundred years, they had remained close to their Dutch roots and traditions. These hard working people were content with the material success that they had achieved and did not share the revolutionary fervor of their English neighbors. Because they lacked enthusiasm for the war, it is often wrongly assumed that Flatbush was loyal to the British. Stiles, for example, characterizes the Dutch as a group "whose sympathies were but slightly enlisted in behalf of the revolutionary cause, and in whom the fear of pecuniary loss and personal inconvenience quite outweighed the more generous impulses of patriotism."

Stiles's statement seems unduly harsh. The situation for the Dutch, particularly in the thinly populated rural areas, was complicated. Charles Andrew Ditmas, in his book *Historic Homesteads of Kings County*, tries to justify the actions of the people under siege:

> I do not think we can blame people for signing an address of loyalty under the same conditions as these people who were compelled to do so or hang, as in some instances they were, or have their property confiscated and they themselves thrown into prison and their wives and children thrown out upon

> the world as paupers. There was the case of my own great-great-grandfather, Nicholas Van Brunt, who refused to sign the oath of allegiance when he was captured, at the time of the Battle of Long Island, and who spent some time in the old provost [jail] for his pains. I think the most patriotic people would have done as most of the inhabitants did.

Ditmas accepts Stiles's assertion that the British brought order to the area and became a high-paying market for the farmers. He believed that these same farmers then recycled the British money to the American cause in the form of loans. Most other writers imply that the money contributed was from silver and gold hidden before the war.

Gertrude Lefferts Vanderbilt disputes Stiles's assertions. She points out that with the exception of Flatlands choosing to stay neutral, the other towns in Kings County, including Flatbush, heeded the call of the Committee of Correspondence and sent delegates to a Provincial Congress in order to select delegates to the Continental Congress. David Clarkson, Adrian Voorhees, Jacobus Vandeventer, and John Vandebilt represented Flatbush.

On the one hand there was an element in Flatbush that was hospitable to the British Governor, William Tryon, and to New York Tory Mayor David Mathews, who sought refuge there. And it was home to notorious traitors such as William Axtell, his brother-in-law Frederick DePeyster, and Johannes Casparus Rubel, co-minister of the Flatbush Dutch Reform Church.

Axtell was a descendant of an old British family. One of his ancestors, Colonel Daniel Axtell, had served in Cromwell's army and after he refused the benefits of "general pardons and obligations," he was beheaded by Charles II. By a fortuitous marriage to the wealthy Margareta de Peyster of New York in the 1770s, he was able to purchase a country estate in Flatbush. His estate, later known as Melrose Hall, was said to be the "best" house in Flatbush. There, he lavishly entertained British officers. While his guests were dining and dancing, below them in dungeons beneath the house patriot prisoners were tortured.

A close friend of Governor Tryon, and as an appointed member of His Majesty's Council, Axtell was one of eleven men who served as a special advisor to the governor. During the war he was given the commission of colonel in General Howe's army, and used his rank and friendship with the governor to become one of the most powerful men in Flatbush. During the occupation he controlled and profited from civilian travel, granted licenses to all public houses, and had his own militia that acted more like a gang of thugs preying on the helpless. At the end of the war Axtell's property was confiscated and sold to American war hero Aquila Giles. Ironically, during the war Giles courted Axtell's sister-in-law and later married her.

On the other hand, however, many of its leading citizens, including David Clarkson and his son David Clarkson Jr., Matthew Clarkson, Abraham E. Lott, and John Lefferts and his son John Lefferts Jr., were unwavering in their support of the Revolution. Others, although they had signed loyalty oaths to the King, risked death to secretly, and at great risk to themselves, provide New York state with specie (gold & silver coin) in support of the Revolution.

Flatbush

As the staging area for part of the battlefield of the Battle of Brooklyn and then as the center of activity during the seven-year occupation of Kings County, Flatbush bore the brunt of the hardships. First, the fighting had left the town in ruins. Houses and fields had been burned, animals driven off, food supplies taken, and personal effects destroyed. Second, with the evacuation of American troops on August 29, 1776, Flatbush became the center of the seven-year occupation during which its previously well-ordered society was reduced to lawlessness and terror. According to Strong:

> As soon as the British had taken possession of New York, and the army had left the Island, the inhabitants of Flatbush began to return. Some were absent only a few days, but others did not reach their homes until nearly mid-winter. The scene presented to the view of those who came back soon after the battle, was distressing indeed. The place where the encampment had been was strewed with feathers, straw, papers and pieces of furniture which had been taken from the houses. In the street, which was grown over with high grass, in consequence of the frequent rains, which occurred at that time, and the interruption of nearly all traveling, were to be seen, in addition to other things, skins of hogs which had been slain, and heads of cattle, with their horns on them, presenting a frightful picture of the haste and waste which had characterized the army. On visiting their houses, they found the greater part of their furniture broken and almost every thing valuable about their premises injured. So wanton had been the waste, that feather beds had not only been ripped up, but in some instances the feathers had been emptied into wells. The best rooms in the houses had been used as stables for the horses, while the drawers in their cupboards and bureaus had served as mangers and feeding troughs. As we may well suppose, the whole town exhibited a scene of wide spread desolation.

The destruction of their property was only the beginning of their troubles. Gertrude Lefferts Vanderbilt, in her book *The Social History of Flatbush*, described the despair:

> There was a great change in the surroundings of the people after the Battle of Flatbush. The withdrawal of Washington's army left the inhabitants so entirely at the mercy of the enemy that there is no doubt that the marjority of them considered the cause hopeless and further resistance useless.

Those people who were suspected of having some loyalty to the Americans were without protection of the laws. They became victims of a rampant lawlessness from petty annoyances such as having fences and farm utensils taken for firewood, to serious thefts such as robbing hen roosts and stealing cattle, hogs, and horses. People were afraid to plow for fear that one of their few remaining horses would be snatched from in front of the plow. Strong tells the story of a British Colonel "L" who tried to take Captain Vandeveer's horses when he was plowing his field:

> The Captain refused to give up his horses and showed his protection order from Captain Dalrymple. This so disconcerted the Colonel, that he was quite enraged, and in a violent manner exclaimed, "You, Flatbushers are always meddling. He went then and seized the horses of Judge Lott and of Judge Vanderbilt, who had no protection.

What was even worse than loss of property, Vanderbilt believed, was "the danger to life and the constant feeling of personal insecurity." And in fact one of the greatest threats to the people came from a band of men that the wealthy loyalist William Axtell organized as a militia. These men, called the "Nassau Blues" but known more familiarly as the "Nasty Blues," regularly terrorized the civilian population.

To add further insult to the injuries already suffered, the British maintained the practice of billeting soldiers and prisoners on the private population, a practice that was so distasteful, some years later it was outlawed by the Third Amendment of the U.S. Constitution. But between 1776 and 1883, when the occupation was in force, and despite dreadful conditions, no householder could refuse. "To make the scanty [food] supply more inadequate," Vanderbilt remarked, "the whole town was filled with soldiers." She continued:

> Some of these were of the roughest class. These were billeted upon the people without their consent, and often in opposition to their express wishes. . . . Even when congress promised two dollars per week, there was very little prospect at that time that it would be paid; and the Continental money which was a legal tender was much depreciated.

In addition to having house guests imposed, even when they were American prisoners of war who had been paroled in Flatbush, there was often a certain amount of class or culture conflict between "guest" and "host." The paroled prisoners who were free to move around the town, provided they reported back to the British at required times, mistrusted their Dutch hosts, who they felt had not done a sufficient amount for the war effort and were probably trying to protect their property in league with the British. The Dutch, who in today's language would be described as traumatized, had in a summer witnessed the destruction of their town, fields, and homes. One catches a glimpse of this tension in the diary of Colonel Graydon, an American prisoner billeted in the home of Jacob Suydam, a descendant of one of the oldest Dutch settler families:

> Lt. Forrest and myself were billeted on Mr. Jacob Suydam, whose house was pretty large, consisting of buildings which appear to have been erected at different times. . . . Though we were generally civilly enough received, it cannot be supposed we were very welcome to our Low Dutch hosts, whose habits were extremely parsimonious and whose winter provision was barely sufficient for themselves. Had they been sure of receiving the $2 per week, it might have reconciled them, Congress or ourselves being looked on as paymasters. They were, however, a people who seemed thoroughly disposed

> to submit to any power that might be imposed on them: and whatever might have been their propensities at an earlier stage of the contest, they were now the dutiful and loyal subjects of His Majesty King George III. Their houses and beds we found clean; but their living extremely poor. A sorry wash made up of a sprinkling of bohea and the darkest sugar on the verge of fluidity, with half-baked bread (fuel being among the scarcest articles at Flatbush) and a little stale butter, constituted our breakfast. At our first coming, a small piece of pickled beef was occasionally boiled for dinner, but to the beef which was soon consumed, there succeeded clippers or clams; and our unvaried supper was supon or mush, sometimes with skimmed milk, but more generally with a buttermilk, blended with molasses, which was kept for weeks in a churn, as swill is saved for hogs. I found it, however, after a little use, very eatable; and supper soon became my best meal. The table company consisted of the master of the house, Mr. Jacob Suydam, an old bachelor; a young man, a shoemaker of the name of Rem Hegeman, married to Jacob's niece, who with a mewling infant in her arms, never failed to appear. A black boy too, was generally in the room; not as a waiter, but a sort of *enfant de maision*, who walked about or took post in the chimney corner with his hat on, and occasionally joined in the conversation. Rem Hegeman, and Yonichy his wife gave themselves no airs; nor was harmony with uncle Jacob ever interrupted; but once, when soured a little, he made a show of knocking down Mr. Forrest with a pair of yarn stocking he had just drawn from his legs, as he sat in the chimney corner one evening preparing for bed; but moments of peevishness were allowed to our host, for we had been consuming his provisions, while he had never seen a penny of our money.

The nadir of the occupation came in the fall of 1776 when an epidemic of camp fever (typhus) swept through Flatbush, caused by the filthy conditions of the town that included dead animals, overcrowding, and new germs brought by soldiers from abroad. The sick and the wounded were taken to the church and several private homes that served as a temporary hospital, but there was no one to treat them. In fact, aggregating the sick only seemed to exacerbate the conditions. Nevertheless town life went on, and even with scarcity ways to help were found.

The women of Flatbush tried to provide relief for the sick and the wounded in the hospital. In addition, the ladies sewing circle made articles for the army including, according to Vanderbilt:

> "1,100 havelocks [a cap cover with a flap at the back to protect the neck from rain or sun]; 312 haversacks; 105 nightshirts; 97 flannelshirts; 500 cotton shirts; 26 dressing gowns (double); 60 pair of knit socks (wool); 161 pairs of drawers; 772 handkerchiefs, plus towels, housewives clothing (not new), lint, old lien, bandages.

There was also a donation of $2,543.99 raised by Flatbush at the Kings County Sanitary Fair.

The significant financial contribution, in silver and gold coin, that the people of Flatbush made to New York state, and which aided Governor George Clinton in pursuing the war, was a most important and heroic service. Had the donors been caught making such loans by the British they would have surely been executed and all their property confiscated. Strong, whose writing in 1842 was closest to the events, probably knew some of the participants and their children. According to him:

> The currency of the country consisted chiefly in the continental paper. This had become so much depreciated, that it was of little value, and it was absolutely essential to the success of the American cause, that specie be obtained. It was therefore contrived to borrow money for the use of the army from the whigs [supporters of the American cause], on the west end of Long Island, who had in their possession large sums of gold and silver. The agent affecting these loans, was Major Hendrick Wyckoff. . . . He was a confidential friend of Governor Clinton, and a brave, discreet and enterprising officer, a man of sterling integrity and honesty. . .

Wyckoff, a direct descendant of Pieter Claesen and a scion of one of the old families, with ties through marriages and friendship to many of the families in Kings County, was well suited to the task. The problem to be worked out first was how did they obtain the money? It was resolved by chance when American prisoner of war Lieutenant Samuel Dodge was billeted with Barent Johnson, a staunch whig. In the course of the imprisonment, it is thought that Johnson suggested the idea of obtaining specie in Kings County as loans to the state. The first loan was given to Colonel Ellison, who obtained £700 from Barent Johnson in December 1777. Once the state recognized it could obtain specie in Kings County, Major Wyckoff became the trusted courier. Strong continues the story:

> It was an enterprise attended with imminent danger, and one which required great skill and secrecy in its execution. The plan usually pursued by the Major, was to cross the sound from Connecticut and conceal himself at Cow Neck. The house in which he usually secreted, was that of Peter Onderdonk, a war friend of the American cause. He [Wyckoff] was entrusted by Governor Clinton, with blank notes, signed by him, which the Major was to fill up to certain individuals, for such sums as he received from them. He had his agents in parts of Kings County, who obtained money for him, and took it to him. Judge Cowenhoven of New Utrecht . . . was one of these. He carried to the Major, the chief part of the money raised for this object, in Flatbush. . . . In effecting this service for his country, Major Wyckoff ran many risks of his life. On one occasion he was concealed for two or more days and nights in a thicket of briar bushes, from which he could see the men who were in pursuit of him.

In 1842 no written records of all the money loaned could be found, although it is said that the state honored all the notes presented. Writing at a later date, Ditmas was able to publish a more complete list of "financiers of the State." Among those who lent money to the state, Strong tells the story:

> of the mother of the present old Mrs. Lefferts . . . [She] advanced 500 pounds or $1250. On one occasion, when counting out the money to the person who was about to take it to Major Wyckoff, a British officer entered the house, and she came near being discovered and apprehended.

Another story Strong tells concerns two prominent gentlemen:

> Captain Cornelius Vanderveer and Judge Lott, united in advancing on a certain occasion a sum of money. The precise amount we know not. But they received the simple note signed by Governor Clinton. To preserve this voucher, they enclosed it in a bottle. This being well corked, they buried it under one of the posts of Mr. Vanderveer's barn. At the close of the war, they dug up the bottle, but on opening it they found all the writing on the note was obliterated, except the signature of George Clinton. When the State repaid the loans, this note among others was presented. The Governor inquired into the cause of it being so defaced, and at first hesitated to honor it. But on being told the circumstances connected with it he honorably discharged it.

It is said that George Martense was the largest lender, believed to have loaned £2,200 pounds, or $5,500, to the cause. The irony is that the British always considered him favorable to their cause and his property had been kept safe. British officers often came to his house and one, Major Moncrief, was quartered there. Over the course of the war approximately $200,000 in specie was loaned, taken from behind British lines. "And what is more remarkable," Strong comments, "not a single person who aided in this business was discovered."

On November 25, 1783, George Washington returned to New York triumphantly. Given the ambivalence of many in Kings County toward the war and the distrust many of the Americans had for the residents of Kings County, in order to firmly establish themselves as loyal citizens, the freeholders and inhabitants of the county addressed the following document to Washington:

> To his Excellency GEORGE WASHINGTON, Esq., General and Commander-in-chief of the armies of the United States of America.
> The ADDRESS of the FREEHOLDERS and INHABITANTS of Kings Co., on Nassau Island (Long Island) in the State of N.Y., who are attached to the freedom and independence of America.

> With hearts full of duty and acknowledgment to the Supreme Director of all human events, and with the most profound respect for your Excellency, we beg leave to present you our sincere congratulations, on this glorious and ever memorable era of the sovereignty and independence of the United States of America, sanctioned by the Definitive Treaty, and the evacuation of the city of N.Y.; your Excellency's entry into which, with his Excellency Gov. Clinton was with such dignity, order and regulation as will redound to the lasting honor of our Excellency, be revered by foreign powers, and certainly obtain the affection of many whose sentiments are averse to that liberty which with the divine assistance your Excellency has so happily acquired for us. Our unfeigned prayers will ever be for your health and happiness, whether you retire to the private paths of peace, or hereafter may be called to move in the busy scenes of war, in the defence [*sic*] of your country. With sincere affection equal duty and respect, we humbly beg leave to subscribe ourselves in behalf of the freeholders and inhabitants of the aforesaid.

With the British gone, life in Flatbush for most people slowly began to return to normal, but with a difference—they began to recognize themselves as Americans—and this became clear a few years later when the town decided to build the Erasmus Academy as a secular school with democratic principles. The people of Flatbush, like those in the other towns of Kings County, embraced the new government. The day they ran their newly made American flag up the new liberty pole erected at the center of town opposite the church, was a great occasion. With the flag's raising, for the first time a symbol of America was displayed in Flatbush—and people celebrated.

Chapter Three

THE VILLAGE OF FLATBUSH

"Now the land is passing out of the hands of its former owners, the old names are disappearing, and the descendants of the first settlers are comparatively few. As long as it was possible to do so, the landowners retained their farms as such; they were not anxious to cut up their beautiful fields into city lots or to widen the green lanes and country roads into dusty avenues and wide boulevards."

—Gertrude Lefferts Vanderbilt
A Social History of Flatbush, 1882

Today, more than one hundred years later, the loss Gertrude Lefferts Vanderbilt (1824–1902) must have felt as she penned those elegiac words is still palpable. Vanderbilt, who was born into one and married into another of Flatbush's oldest and most prominent families, was the author of *The Social History of Flatbush*, a historian of old Dutch traditions, and a collector of old Flatbush stories. Probably nobody had a better understanding of the character and personages of nineteenth-century Flatbush than she.

Through her book Vanderbilt attempted to preserve the memory of a pioneering community, one that faced many hardships, achieved great success, and suffered painful loss. The town's recent memory had been devastated by war and occupation. To its credit, the town rebounded quickly and went on to rebuild. Nevertheless, Vanderbilt recognized that in spite of its resiliency, stability, and strength, the world she knew and loved could not survive the forces of modernization and urbanization overtaking it.

The Flatbush vanishing before her eyes was a tight-knit community deeply rooted in land held by the same families for generations. Records going back nearly 250 years from the date she wrote *The Socical history of Flatbush* show that when land was transferred, the sale was often within the extended family or to a near neighbor. There are several reasons why Flatbush had been successful and stable.

First was its location at the center of Kings County. Since the seventeenth century it had been a hub of economic, educational, religious, and political activity. Second was its physical layout. Flatbush was built with most of its houses along the east and west sides of Flatbush Road or Main Street (today's Flatbush Avenue), with their fields situated behind them. This created a town life and avoided the isolation that is often the lot of farmers. The third reason was the liberal Dutch social traditions of the period that tolerated diversity and encouraged a public spiritedness that infused the town. And finally, perhaps the most important reason was the frequent intermarriage among the land-owning families. This created a deep and complex social web of kinship ties that not only held Flatbush together, but also, in spite of some spats and lawsuits, bonded it to the other towns in the area, particularly Flatlands.

Vanderbilt anticipated the dizzying transformation that within a period of less than twenty years would change Flatbush from a sparsely populated rural town ruled by tradition, gently enforced by a social elite, to a thriving urban village that bore no resemblance to its pastoral past. Measured by population growth, Flatbush grew from a village of approximately 941 people in 1790, the year of the first United States Census, to 3,177 people in 1850. The next census in 1860 (after the town of New Lots, also known as East Flatbush, separated from it), showed that Flatbush had only slightly increased its population to 3,471 persons. Ten years later, at the end of the Civil War, the 1870 census shows that the population had just about doubled to 6,309 persons. This marked the beginning of the town's transition from a farming center into a suburban community. In 1890, the last year independent census figures existed for the town of Flatbush, the population was 12,338, more than six times what it had been fifty years earlier. In 1894 Flabush ended its resistance to annexation by Brooklyn and ceased to be an independent entity. On January 1, 1898, Manhattan, Brooklyn, the Bronx, Queens, and Staten Island became the five boroughs of the City of Greater New York and Flatbush became a neighborhood of that city. By 1910 almost all vestiges of the rural town had vanished. Flatbush Avenue had become a thriving commercial street, most of the old farmhouses that had lined it had been torn down, and the farms subdivided and sold to real estate developers. It is not surprising that the settlement of Mrs.Vanderbilt's estate in 1905 included the sale of her home and land at 560 Flatbush Avenue (near Lincoln Road) to Lester Realty Company, a developer, for the then handsome price of $150,000.

Building the Erasmus Hall Academy and the Rebirth of Flatbush

In 1783 the British, who had occupied Flatbush since August 1776, withdrew their troops, leaving behind a town politically divided and physically destroyed. Houses and barns had been burned, possessions looted, and the once neat, prosperous farms were in ruin. All of this had to be rebuilt, and the political tension between the American patriots and the pro-British loyalists that had roiled the town had to end. Raising the liberty pole had been a first step in what became the rapid embrace by residents of citizenship in a new free and independent United States of America. Still, the old town life had been irreversibly altered and more changes were to come.

If at the end of the war the future seemed bleak to some, others recognized in spite of all that happened Flatbush still had its community and culture. Although Flatbush and its sister towns in rural Kings County were among the American communities that had borne the heaviest brunt of the war and suffered great devastation, the people endured. Through it all, the human infrastructure—the social order that had been maintained through family ties and long time friendships—may have been shaken, but the British had not broken it. The public spiritedness that had earlier characterized the town remained. People rebuilt their houses and farms, and most important, the town's leaders were ready to take on public works.

A major project was to rebuild the church, which due to structural flaws was in serious disrepair (see chapter one). Construction of the new building, which is still in use today, was begun in 1793 and completed in 1796. The first new undertaking, however, was to build a school. Construction of the Erasmus Hall Academy, named for the sixteenth-century Dutch philosopher and humanist Desiderius Erasmus, began in 1787, the year that the U.S. Constitution was adopted. The community intended it to be a secular institution to celebrate the new democratic principles that now governed their lives, including the principle of separation of church and state. Until then, the town school was church-affiliated. Nevertheless, through most of its history as a private academy, a clergyman was at its helm. Under the leadership of Judge John Vanderbilt, who became the first chairman of its board, and the Reverend Dr. John H. Livingston, a well respected educator, theologian, and scholar, who became its first principal, Erasmus Hall Academy would become one of the ground-breaking schools that led the evolution of secondary education in New York state; its curriculum, a mixture of classical and practical education, a model for other schools to follow. And as its founders intended, it was also an important element in the revitalization of Flatbush. Not only did it bring new activity and new energy to the town, it established Flatbush as a center of learning and served as an instrument of change. From the day it opened almost all the children of Flatbush were educated there. Many of them went on to college and professional life.

With the support of the Flatbush elite, most descendants of the early families, a subscription paper was circulated first within the town and then to friends throughout the area. Vanderbilt, the largest donor, headed the list, pledging £100. Aaron Burr and Alexander Hamilton, not Flatbush residents, pledged £10 each. The new building stood on Flatbush Avenue opposite the church on land that had been given by the church. It had a frontage of one hundred feet and a depth of thirty-six feet. When completed it cost $6,250, substantially more than the money raised in the subscription. In order to clear the debt, the town decided to sell Corlear and Twillers Flats, large tracts of land that had been the first purchased in Flatbush and still held in common by the proprietors of the town. The land was sold for $16 per acre. Many residents of Flatbush entitled to a share of the proceeds donated them to the academy and these donations added $1,500 to the building fund.

The rest of the money was divided among Flatbush residents who had refused to relinquish their share for the academy. For the most part these were people who had maintained their allegiance to the old church-run village school and opposed the new academy. They had tried to stop the academy from being built by discouraging subscriptions. To illustrate the vehemence of their opposition, Reverend Strong in his book *The History of Flatbush* tells this story, "One worthy old gentleman, when unloading some bags, unfortunately slipped, and fell from his waggon [*sic*]. He rose greatly incensed, and cried out, 'that Academy will never do.' "

In May 1787 the founders applied to the regents of the University of the State of New York for a charter. It was granted on November 20, 1787, making Erasmus Hall the first school of secondary education to be granted a charter by the newly formed state regents. The founding trustees, most of whom were from the oldest Flatbush families were John Vanderbilt, Walter Minto, Peter Lefferts, Johannes E. Lott, Aquila Giles, Cornelius Vanderveer, George Martense, Jacob Lefferts, William B. Gifford, Hendrick Suydam, Martinus Schoonmaker, John J. Vanderbilt, Philip Nagel, Peter Cornell, and John H. Livingston. Four of the trustees, James Wilson, Samuel Provost, John Mason, and Comfort Sands, were not residents of Flatbush and did not participate. They were soon replaced by Reverend Peter Lowe, Garrit Martense, Peter Stryker, and Cornelius Bergen.

The trustees succeeded in establishing a first-class institution that employed instructors who were leading scholars of the day. As a private academy the school charged tuition. At first tuition was £6 and the entrance fee was one guinea for all departments except English. English instruction was £3 10 shillings and a one-half guinea entrance fee. Nevertheless, tuition was never sufficient to cover costs. The trustees were under the constant pressure—still faced by their modern-day counterparts of eleemosynary institutions—of keeping the institution solvent and alive, carrying out their educational mission, and paying for it. It took the trustees until May 1825 to fully discharge the building debt. Throughout the life of the Hall, meeting its budgetary needs remained a problem.

Erasmus Hall was given a strong start by its first principal, Dr. Reverend John H. Livingston, a prominent church scholar who was then the first and only professor of theology for the Reformed Dutch Church in America. Dr. Livingston, a descendant of the powerful Livingston family of Eastern New York, attended Yale University where he earned his bachelors and masters degrees. He then went to Holland where he earned his Doctor of Divinity from the University of Utrecht. He served, without remuneration, as principal of Erasmus Hall from 1787 to 1792, when he resigned. Although Dr. Livingston was not responsible for day-to-day classroom activity, he was more than a figurehead. He took an active role in the selection of teachers and closely supervised their work although the burden of supervising students and maintaining the academic program was the responsibility of the first teacher and of the various departments. Until 1814 being the principal of Erasmus Hall Academy carried no instructional duties.

It is apparent from his letter of resignation that Dr. Livingston had two motives for accepting the position at the academy. The first was to help launch it because he sincerely believed in its educational goals. The second was he expected the new Dutch Reform Theological Seminary, of which he was the only professor, would be located in Flatbush. Explaining his first reason, Livingston said:

> I am now happy in seeing the prosperity of an academy whose welfare lies so near my heart; and as the great end for which I consented to be your Principal appears to be fully obtained, I conceive it to be proper to communicate to the Board of Trustees by this letter that I wish to resign to them the office.

However, Dr. Livingston and the town of Flatbush were disappointed when the General Synod of the Reformed Dutch Church decided against building its new seminary in Flatbush as it had originally planned. Instead the seminary became a department at Rutgers University in New Jersey. Accordingly, Dr. Livingston then accepted the position of professor of Theology at Rutgers and eventually became the president of the university. Reverend Strong, commenting on the loss, called the move "regrettable," saying that had the seminary:

> been continued in Flatbush, Erasmus would long ere this, have grown into a flourishing college, under the auspices of the State of New York, and the literary as well as the theological interests of the Reformed Dutch Church, have been prospered in a far higher degree that they have yet been.

In 1788, the first year of Dr. Livingston's tenure as principal of Erasmus Hall, the board of trustees devised a set of rules governing both academic standards and personal conduct at Erasmus Hall. Although the code went into great detail on all aspects of faculty and student life at the Hall, what is particularly interesting is the organization of the academic departments and the responsibilities of the teachers:

> The number of teachers in the Hall will depend upon the number of students, but there shall be constantly two departments at least supplied with competent and able teachers.
>
> The first department is the Classical, in which the Latin and Greek languages shall be taught and to which Geography shall be annexed.
>
> The second depart is the English, in which Reading, English, the English Grammar, Writing, Arithmetic and Bookkeeping are comprehended.
>
> The teachers in both departments shall mutually assist each other as far as their diligent attention to their own respective branches will permit, and shall always unite in promoting the reputation and prosperity of the Hall to their utmost ability.
>
> The teacher in the Classical Department is the first in rank, and shall have a right to inspect the progress of all the students in their respective branches as often as he shall judge necessary, unless the Principal shall otherwise direct.

Quarterly examinations, attended by the trustees, the principal of the school, the faculty, and whatever members of the community at large cared to attend, were an important aspect of the program. As part of the examination students were required to deliver orations, or sometimes participate in debates. In addition, teachers were encouraged to give frequent exams at their discretion.

The most rules, however, applied to student conduct and were intended to keep students on their best behavior. These rules ran the gamut: on the one hand were the "don'ts," for example one rule forbade the typical hijinks of high-spirited young people:

drinking, gambling, and "profane swearing;" on the other hand were the "do's," for example, a rule that required attendance at daily public prayer services, morning and evening at the Hall, and other "proper" behaviors.

The scholar, who at Dr. Livingston's suggestion succeeded him, was Dr. Peter Wilson. Dr. Wilson had resigned his post as a professor of Greek and Latin at Columbia College in order to take the position of first teacher in 1792. He was paid what was considered at that time a handsome salary of £400 per year. Shortly after his arrival he was elected principal after Dr. Livingston resigned. Wilson held the position from 1792 to 1804 when he resigned to return to Columbia College. During the tenures of Livingston and Wilson the school grew, attracting young men from other states, mostly in the south and from other countries. In order to house these students many Flatbush families agreed to take them as boarders, charging them £20 per year.

Early in the administration of Jonathan W. Kellogg, who served as principal from 1823 to 1834, separate facilities for male and female students were introduced and female instructors were hired to teach the girls. Up to that point boys and girls attended the same classes and were taught by the same instructors. The division included separate boys' and girls' entrances and classrooms.

Over the years Erasmus Hall graduated many people who went on to hold important posts. In the nineteenth century these included William A. Duer, who became president of Columbia College; John Berrian, who served as attorney general of the United States and in 1842 was a member of the U.S. Senate from Georgia; George M. Troup, who served several terms as governor of Georgia; John Hunter, elected to the New York state senate; Reverend Jno. Blair Linn, minister of the Reformed Dutch Church of New York and a distinguished American poet; Morris Miller, who served in Congress before becoming first judge of Oneida County, New York; as well as many men who became ministers and served congregations throughout the northeast.

On June 16 and 17, 1887 Erasmus Hall celebrated its one-hundreth birthday in grand style with festivities, speeches, and remembrances of former students. Of all the presentations, the remembrances by Mrs.Vanderbilt's most caught the spirit of the school and its times. Vanderbilt had had a long association with the school through family and as a student. Her father John Lefferts served on the board from 1807 to his death in 1829; her husband, Judge John Vanderbilt, served from 1841–1877, when he died; and her son Lefferts Vanderbilt became a trustee in 1878 and served until 1895.

Gertrude Lefferts Vanderbilt attended the Hall almost fifty years earlier, when John Kellogg and later Dr. William H. Campbell had been the principal. And while admitting that her memory may have been colored by nostalgia and the passage of time, the reminiscences of this astute observer of Flatbush life draw us into the world of a school girl long ago:

> With all the congratulations presented on this pleasant occasion, we mothers who were once children here wish also to add our greeting. We who have sons and daughters to take our places can recall many pleasant memories of the days spent at school in Erasmus Hall, our alma mater as

well as yours. Accepting the privilege accorded us, we would add our quota by introducing the social element in the form of some reminiscences of the girls' school-room. Life being in the decline with us, there may be a sunset glow thrown over these memories irradiating them with brighter colors than were theirs at the dawn. Some of us present to-night (now past the meridian of life) may go back as far as when Mr. Kellog entered our names on his roll-book as children in his primary department. Age and this are marked with differences every step of the way, and the changes 'twixt now and then challenge a contrast from the very beginning, for those were the days of quill pens. Steel pens formed no part of our school outfit.

A neat bundle of goose quills always had their place on the teacher's desk. . . . He [Mr. Kellogg] was always pleasant and gentle; ever ready with his sharp penknife to mend a sputtering quill or to accept it as an excuse for poor penmanship or for want of neatness in a copy-book. In those days we walked to school through the rural beauty of the village street, sometimes loitering under the shade trees, sometimes hurrying as we heard the tinkle of the cowbell as the herd were driven home from pasture and we were afraid to pass some dilatory animal that lingered to graze on the sidewalk. On rainy days no public conveyance gave us the facility now offered to reach school at the cost of five cents. Some accommodating parent harnessed up his horses, and the wagon stopped and took in all the neighbors' children who lived on the way. As a means of heating the houses furnaces were then unknown. Our schoolrooms were heated by cast-iron stoves. We can recall one of these in a recitation room. Curiously enough it had an oven in it with two doors opening out on either side. The class sat close to this stove—half on one side and half on the other. The French teacher often wondered why the covers of our books were so scorched. It would not be telling tales out of school at this late hour to explain how it happened; but perhaps it might betray the stratagems of their grandparents when lessons were not properly committed to memory. I am free to admit, however, that there is very little in this direction that we could teach the children of the present day. . . . The boys had a yearly exhibition, and on that occasion a platform was erected in front of the pulpit in the church. We thought our brothers and cousins and young friends who spoke upon the platform as eloquent as ever Webster or Clay might have been. We expected them in after years to fill the highest places of honor that the nation could bestow. Nothing less than public recognition from the Mississippi to the Atlantic Coast was considered to be their just due. At one of these exhibitions instead of selections from the celebrated orators and poets of the world the boys were taught to take sides in a discussion on the character of Napoleon Bonaparte. . . . Among our teachers we recall with affectionate respect Dr. Campbell.

Continued on page 97

ayment to Sachem Eskemoppas and his brothers Kinnarimas and Ahawaham

) Fathoms of black seewant or wampum
) Fathoms of white seewant or wampum
Matched coats or Duffells
Blankets
Gunners sight guns
Pistols
Double handfuls of Powder
5 Bars of lead
10 Knives
2 Secret Aprons of Duffells, (Cuppas of Duffell)
1 Half fat or half barrel of Strong Beer
3 Cans Brandy
6 Shirts

ne residents of Flatbush, represented by Adrian Hegeman, Jacob Stryker, Hendrich Joris, and Jan Hansen, reed to pay Eskemoppas and his brothers these items for the deed to Flatbush. The Dutch believed this as an unfair claim since they had earlier purchased the land from the Canarsee Indians and had various tents attesting to their ownership. However, the town believed it was more prudent to remake the rchase. The deed was signed and delivered in the presence of Thomas Lovelace and Cornelius Van uyven and recorded by Mathias Nicolls, secretary. John Manning, Sylvester Salisbury, John Hough, cob Van Cortlandt, Teunis Jacob Hay, and Edward Carlisle, the latter three believed to be judges or stices of the peace, witnessed the delivery of the items. As required, Sachem Eskemoppas and his brothers knowledged their satisfaction with the exchange before Governor Francis Lovelace.

om Thomas M. Strong, *History of the Town of Flatbush in Kings County*, 1842.

See page 9

Contributions to Church Building Fund

To the building received from:	Guilders*	Stivers*
Fort Orange	90	
Esopus	50	
New Amsterdam	1,876	3
Gowanus	35	10
Brooklyn	112	10
Amersfoort (Flatlands)	120	
New Utrecht	17	10
Midwout (Flatbush)	427	
E. (probably India) Company	588	
The first preaching (collection probably)	90	
Hon. Fiscal, or Attorney General	30	
Also in addition	113	
Marriage Fees	43	
Hempstead, by bequest	50	

*Guilders or Florins = 20 Stivers/ Stivers=1/20th Guilder

From Thomas M. Strong, *History of the Town of Flatbush in Kings County, L.I.* 1842

See page 24

The Reverend Bernardus Freeman, whose calling to minister the Dutch Reform Church of Flatbush created a thirteen-year rift in the congregation. As a result he shared the pulpit with a second minister, the Reverend Vicentius Antonides. Freeman served from 1705 to his death in 1741.

The home of the Reverend Bernardus Freeman, minister of the First Dutch Reform Church. It later passed on to David Clarkson, and it was here during the American Revolution that the British had a drunken orgy drinking Clarkson's rare wines. The house, which stood on the northwest corner of Flatbush Avenue and Albemarle Road, was later owned by the Bergen family, and was demolished in 1891.

The Dutch Reform Church at the beginning of the nineteenth century.

Learning to quilt, one of the many activities teaching the crafts of long ago at Lefferts House. The tall chest in the background is a Kas, one of the most important pieces of Dutch furniture, used to store linens and other valuable household goods.

The Reverend Ulpianus Van Sinderen. A staunch patriot, he served during the American Revolution.

It was at the Vechhte-Cortelyou house or old stone house in Gowanus (c. 1776) that the final battle in the Battle of Brooklyn was fought. The brave actions of Lord Stirling and the Marylanders, against overwhelming odds, made it possible for many Americans to escape. More than 250 Marylanders were lost or captured, including Lord Stirling who surrendered himself to the Hessians.

On August 27, 1776 the Battle of Long Island, the first and largest engagement of the American Revolution, took place on this site. At that time the greatly out numbered,rag-tag American army faced well organized British and Hessian troops. As he viewed the battle from Cobble Hill a short distance away, George Washington is said to have cried out in anguish, "Good God! What brave fellows I must lose this day." The battle was lost, but fortunately, the Americans and George Washington were able to escape to fight another day. This 2001 reenactment took place on what is now Prospect Park's long meadow. (Photo by Igou Allbray.)

Battle Pass, 1776.

The retreat of the American troops under General Stirling across Gowanus Creek during the Battle of Long Island. Engraving after a painting by Alonzo Chappel. From A History of Long Island, *Volume I (1902), by Peter Ross.*

Captain Vanderveer and other men of Flatbush engaged in a skirmish with the British a few days before the battle of Brooklyn but were repulsed by hastily constructed British fortifications. When Vanderveer returned home he found his house in the hands of the enemy. Still in uniform, he was captured and narrowly avoided being hanged. A British officer with whom he was acquainted obtained a "protection" for him from General Cornwallis. Vanderveer accepted the protection and agreed to go back to his farm on the condition he not be asked to fight against his country. During the war Captain Vanderveer was one of the Flatbush residents who loaned money for the war effort to Governor Clinton. The Vanderveer homestead stood on Flatbush Avenue between Avenue D and Clarendon road until 1911. The house was said to date to 1747.

The Eagle Monument at the site of the Dongon Oak. The plaque reads:

> *At the Battle of Long Island on the hills to the north of this spot, the Americans had a redoubt with 2 guns to guard the old Valley Grove road, called by the old settlers the "porte" meaning gate-way through the hills which ran in front of this monument. By that road stood a white-oak mentioned in the patent of Governor Dongon, November 12, 1685, as a marker between Flatbush and Brooklyn. This tree was cut down and thrown across the road. With the dense wood on the south and the swamps on the north, it made an important obstruction.*
>
> *American Commander General Sullivan valiantly defended this position against the Hessian General De Heister, until attacked from the rear by the British troops under General Clinton. Then they retreated in good order bringing off their artillery.*

About the monument: This monument stands in Prospect Park almost opposite the boulder marking Battle Pass. It was dedicated November 25, 1922. It was commissioned by the St. Nicholas Society, which paid $2,000 for it. The sculptor of the original eagle that sits atop the stone column was Frederick Ruckstall (1853–1942). The eagle was stolen in 1974 and was replaced in 1991 with a similar bronze eagle atop the stone column. The new eagle was based on photos of the original. The sculptor was John Metrovics.

Still following the original path, the American troops march toward the Stone House at Gowanus. (Photo by Igou Allbray.)

On the night before the Battle of Brooklyn the proprietor of Howard's Inn, who sided with the Americans, had some unwelcome British visitors. At gunpoint, he was forced by General Clinton to help get British troops behind the American lines at the unguarded Jamaica Pass.

Vanderveer's Mill, built in 1801 on Flatbush Avenue between Canarsie Lane Paerdegat Road.

Home of Gertrude Lefferts Vanderbilt.

John Lefferts (1826–1893) was the younger brother of Gertrude Lefferts Vanderbilt.

The Mowatt House (c. 1842), home to James and Cora Ann Mowatt, an actress and writer. The house was originally known as Melrose Hall, the home of the Revolutionary War traitor Colonel William Axtell.

In 1875 after they defeated the City of Brooklyn's attempt to annex them, the people of the Town of Flatbush built this town hall to celebrate their victory. That victory was short lived though,because in 1894 the town was annexed by Brooklyn. (Photo by Igou Allbray.)

John Vanderbilt, husband of Gertrude Lefferts Vanderbilt.

The Martense Story House located in the area of today's Parade Grounds on land that belonged to Martin de Boer (Martin the farmer) who was once the largest landholder in Flatbush. The last of the Martense descendants to live in the house was Rachel Martense who was born in 1801 and died in 1905, the oldest resident of Flatbush. According to the story Martense never married because of a sad love affair in her youth. She is described as a charitable woman who even in old age would sew garments for the poor.

The second church built in Flatbush by its growing English population was St. Paul's Protestant Episcopal Church, incorporated in 1836. The original building was wood. In 1902 it was replaced by a much larger stone building designed by the architect Herbert Brewster. That building is still in use.

Lefferts House at its original location on Flatbush Avenue before 1882. The house was given to New York City as a museum house in 1918 and moved to its present site in Prospect Park.

The Willink Mansion c. *1842. The Willink family, newcomers to nineteenth century Flatbush, were a reclusive group who isolated themselves within the mansion they built at the northern end of the town. Today the land is part of Prospect Park.*

Erasmus Hall Academy c. *1842.*

Erasmus Hall High School.

Laying the cornerstone for Erasmus Hall High School, c. *1900.*

Fire drill at the Erasmus Hall Academy. Flatbush Avenue is seen in the background. The Jeremiah Lott house is on the left and the Dr. Newton Ferris house is on the right.

The seal of Erasmus Hall, "Custode Dea Crescet," was adopted in 1787.

The partially completed Erasmus Hall High School early in the twentieth century.

All Souls Universalist Church, c. *1905. This church was one of the most ardent boosters of Flatbush.*

In 1919 sheep still grazed in the Prospect Park meadow.

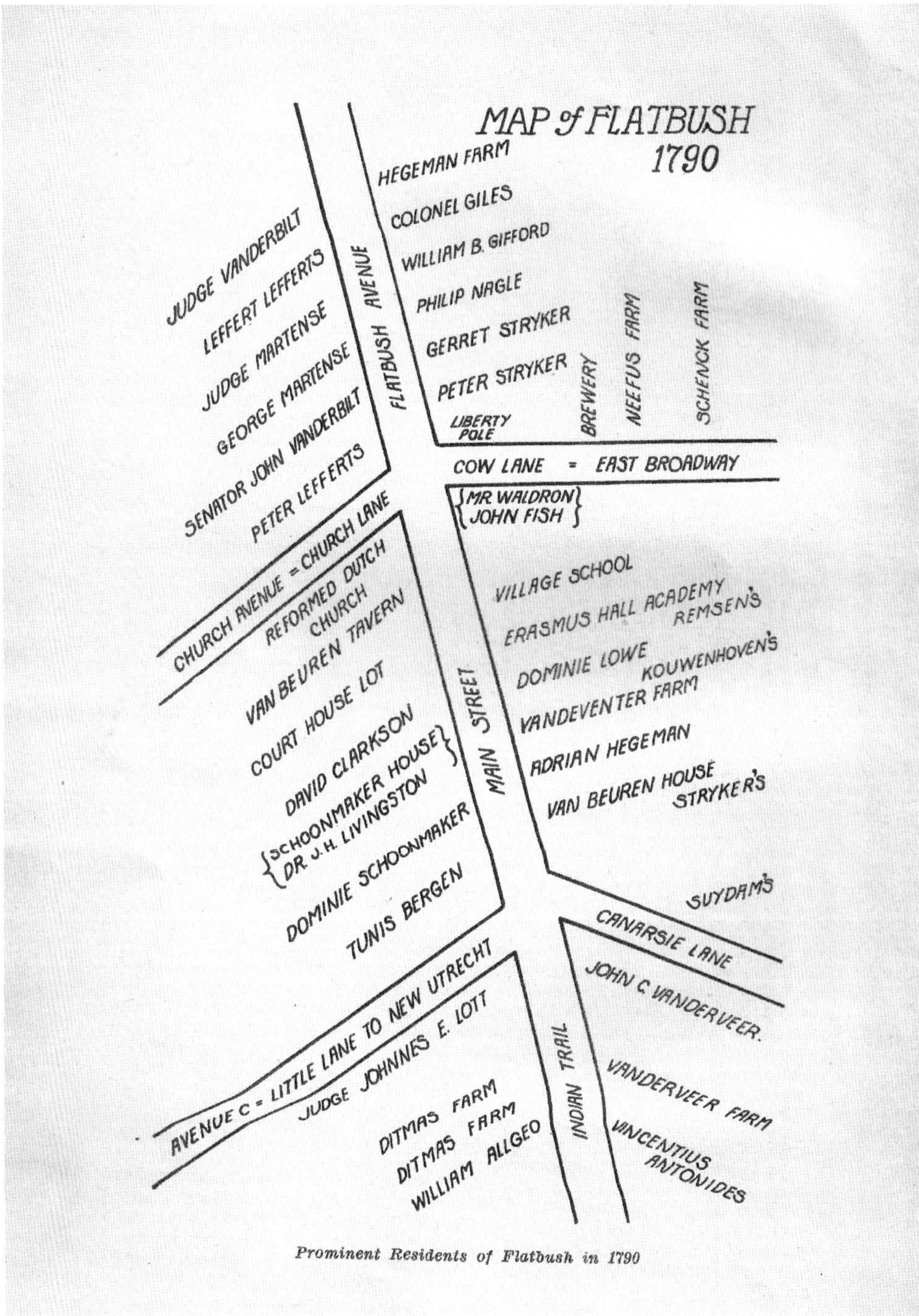

A map showing the location of Flatbush's most prominent families in 1790.

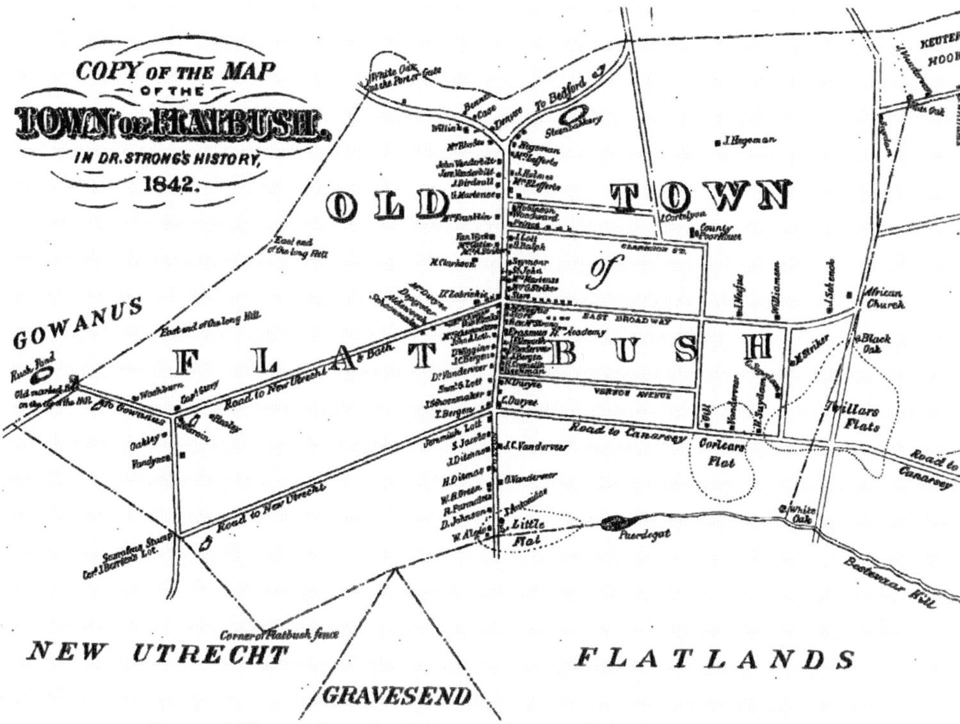

Reverend Thomas Strong's 1842 map showing all the families of Flatbush,

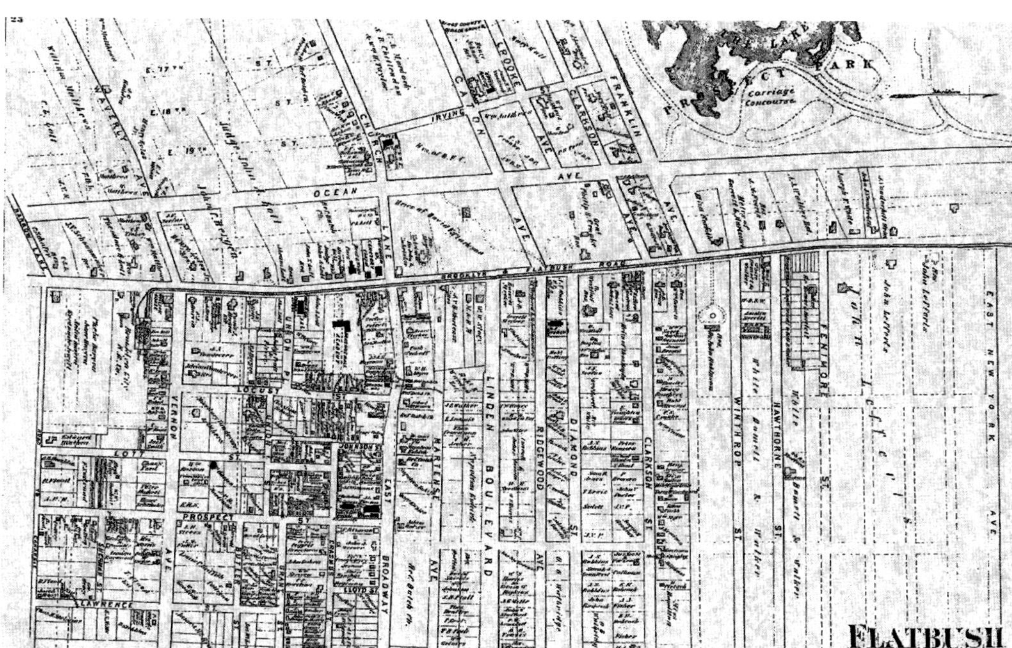

This c. 1873 map shows Flatbush in the early stages of transition from a rural to urban community.

Map of Victorian Flatbush neighborhoods (Map by Rex Curry, courtesy of the Flatbush Development Corporation.)

Dean Alvord, the developer of Prospect Park South.

John Petit designed this Prospect Park South Colonial Revival house in 1900. The paneled dining room, with its dark wood mantle and built-in cupboards, is original. The mural that circles the room was painted by a WPA artist in the 1930s. It depicts a pastoral scene, perhaps the artist's idea of the earlier Flatbush. (Photo by Igou Allbray.)

The first Flatbush-Tomkins Congregational Church was an eight-sided shingled structure designed by the architectural firm Whitefield and King. In 1910 it was replaced by the present building, designed by Francis R. Allen and Charles Collens of Manhattan, and local architect Louis Jallade. It is considered one of the city's finest examples of New Georgian church architecture. Today it is a center of community activity and is the starting point for the annual Victorian Flatbush House Tour.

An ad, c. 1905, for the Ackerson houses in Fiske Terrace. (Courtesy of Mary Kay Gallagher.)

The Knickerbocker Field Club, founded early in the twentieth century, was one of three important social clubs in Flatbush. Although the field house was destroyed by fire, it continues as a tennis club.

The Real Estate office (C. *1916) was located at the edge of Prospect Park South on Coney Island Avenue between Church Avenue and Albemarle Road. (Courtesy Mary Kay Gallagher.)*

Looking north on Buckingham Road C. *1916. The second house is the famous Japanese House that was built to look like a Japanese temple. In front of the truck the street becomes wider to accommodate the planted mall. (Courtesy Mary Kay Gallagher.)*

Looking south up Marlborough Road from Albemarle Road, c. *1916. In Prospect Park South young Norway maples were purposely planted at forty-foot intervals along the property line and away from the curbs in order to make the streets seem broader and shadier. Today, one hundred years later, the trees are reaching the end of their life and many have been cut down. (Courtesy Mary Kay Gallagher.)*

Typical pre–World War II high rise apartment house along Ocean Avenue. The high rise buildings after the war were much starker brick with no ornamentation. (Courtesy of the Flatbush Development Corporation.)

The Avenue H station was saved from the wrecker's ball by community vigilance and in June 2004 was designated a New York City landmark. The wooden station, built in 1909, is the first elevated stop on the southbound Brighton local. The structure was built at the same time as the surrounding Victorian neighborhood of Fiske Terrace, and served as the T.B. Ackerson Company's sales office. Several years ago the Metropolitan Transit Authority declared the station a fire hazard because of its wooden construction and announced that it planned to replace it with a more modern building. The community of Fiske Terrace, supported by the communities of Victorian Flatbush and preservationists throughout the city, strenuously objected. Thousands of people signed petitions in support of keeping the station. It was pointed out that the station, tucked away in a quiet corner of Flatbush, faced no imminent danger of fire and should be preserved as part of the architectural heritage of the subway system and of the community that it serves. Its designation as a landmark guarantees that the station will survive.

Flatbush Avenue c. 1905. Flatbush Avenue was indicative of the rapid changes that swept through Flatbush at the turn of the twentieth century. In a few short years the street changed from a quiet country lane bordered by comfortable homes into a busy urban thoroughfare.

Two views of the interior of a Victorian Flatbush home in the early twentieth century.

Laying the track on the BMT line. Between the Prospect Park station on the north and the Newkirk Avenue station on the south the Q local and B express trains run in an open sunken trench. (Courtesy of the Flatbush Development Corporation.)

In the late 1960s and early 1970s many young, mostly professional families began to move back to Victorian Flatbush. They were delighted to discover the spacious old houses in a dynamic multi-racial, multi-ethnic community. It was a time of community building and getting to know one's neighbors. This softball game, played in Prospect Park in 1979, is affectionately remembered by all who participated, many of whom still live in Victorian Flatbush. (Photo by Anna Budd, courtesy of the Flatbush Development Corp.)

A soccer game on the newly refurbished Parade Grounds.

The Japanese house in Prospect Park South, one of the most famous of the many architecturally varied buildings that are the hallmarks of Victorian Flatbush. (Courtesy Prospect Park South Association.)

The neighborhoods of Victorian Flatbush are often used by film companies to provide the settings for feature films, television, and advertising. Shown is the filming of Sophie's Choice *in Prospect Park South in 1982. Sharing the limelight with the stars Meryl Streep, Kevin Kline, and Peter MacNicol was the shocking pink house. The house is still there but is painted a more conservative gray. (Courtesy Dr. David Kliot.)*

Neighborhood Clean up. (Courtesy of the Flatbush Development Corporation.)

Cleaning graffiti from the overpass at the Beverly Road station. (Courtesy of the Flatbush Development Corporation.)

After almost one hundred years Newkirk Plaza, one of the oldest outdoor shopping malls, is getting a facelift. The Newkirk Avenue Station of the Brighton Line subway runs below in an open cut and stores line both sides. The renovations, done under the auspices of the Flatbush Development Corporation, include new fencing specially developed for the site and decorative paving. In addition to attracting more local shoppers it is hoped that the space will be a gathering place for the community.

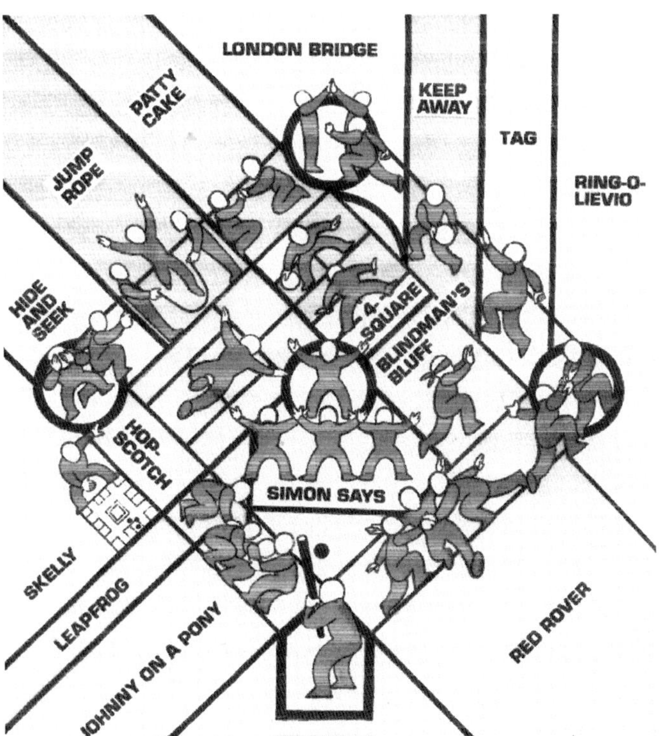

The flyer advertising the Flatbush Frolic XIV Street Fair, sponsored by the Flatbush Development Corporation, recalls the old street games that were once played throughout Flatbush.

Continued from page 64

We look up to him, however, with something like awe because it was whispered among us that he could speak in Latin, Greek and Hebrew just as easily as he could in English. We also recall Professor Mark Hopkins Beecher, who among other things taught us botany and took his class out in the woods botanizing [*sic*]. As on these occasions we begged for the tin cake boxes from the pantries in which to collect our specimens (and carry cake). These botanizing excursions were not as popular with our parents as with ourselves. We were delighted with the tramp through the woods which this method of acquiring knowledge afforded us. And here again is a contrast between past and present, for Flatbush was encircled with woods then. Now chestnut, oak and hickory have disappeared like the frailest wild flowers they sheltered. This being before the days of sewing machines, one afternoon in the week we were taught to sew. It is a good thing for girls to learn. I commend it to teachers of the present day. In order to combine this with mental improvement some one read aloud to us. I fear we did not appreciate this surreptitious method of hindering us from whispering while engaging in sewing. It was not a very varied menu from which our minds were daily fed. The books (which you may still find on top shelves of old closets) are a little antiquated now. The geographies did not tell us much of the country west of the Mississippi River, and our maps left blank and empty spaces where now there are thriving states and great cities. We studied algebra and geometry, rhetoric, Kames's Elements of Criticism, history both ancient and modern. The history of the United States scarcely brought us into the days of Martin Van Buren. Just think how much that leaves untold. With many sighs and tears we struggled over the writing of compositions. We do not wonder now at the tears when we remember that we children were expected to write criticisms on Young's Night Thoughts, Pollock's Course of Time, or Harvey's Meditations, with now and then a review of Paradise Lost.

Erasmus Hall library was to us a place full of wonders, for besides the books there were glass cases filled with natural curiosities, bugs, beetles and lizards preserved in alcohol: weapons from the Cannibal Islands; ornaments worn by natives of the South Sea Islands, and mineralogical specimens from the far West of Ohio and Illinois. There was nothing there from Japan, and the fact marks another stride forward in history, for where now do you find shelves which are not filled with curios from Japan? There were also in the library, glass retorts and all sorts of instruments for experiments in chemistry—in fact, quite a laboratory. We had frequent lectures on chemistry and natural philosophy during the winter . . . and lectures were held in high estimation then as a valuable means of instruction. The wonders shown by means of the glass cylinders and retorts seemed to us children like nothing short of necromancy. . . . We sometimes had lectures on astronomy illustrated by an orrery, in which Jupiter and Saturn and all

> the planets in their turn were suspended from the ceiling and spun around the sun in a very creditable manner, unless, as sometimes happened, some moon got a little refractory and accompanied the wrong planet, or Mars got in undue haste and usurped the orbit of some other world. Had the great solar system acted upon the same erratic principle, I fear that today we should not have a world in which to keep the centennial of Erasmus Hall. We took books weekly out of the library and read them faithfully. Owing to the various chemicals kept in that room the books eventually were permeated by a peculiar odor which became associated in our minds with histories and biographies, so that when about this time a teacher giving us a biographical sketch of some old worthy, remarked that he died "in the odor of sanctity" we thought that of course we understood perfectly what was meant by the phrase. The old library made it plain to us; yes, we knew. Oh the simplicity of little children!
>
> In a school where there were boys and girls studying together a little flirting was very harmless and innocent, and we all know of some happy marriages in which the acquaintance began in the companionship in the school. Beside secular instruction, our religious training was not forgotten. The school was opened by religious exercises, and on our way home Thursday afternoons, we were gathered in the old consistory rooms to repeat our catechism to our beloved pastor Rev. Dr. Strong. These catechetical exercises were considered as important as other studies and we were reprimanded if we failed to attend. While we admit that the old forms of instruction have been superseded by newer and better methods, yet we feel that the minds of the children were less taxed then, and there was a slower and more natural unfolding and ripening of the faculties, so that our girls seemed to retain longer the sweetness and simplicity of their childhood. When we look upon the gray-haired matrons who are here among the happy groups of their children tonight, we can scarcely realize that these are they to whom we have alluded as school-girls. . . . We rejoice that our sons and daughters have had the opportunities which this school has afforded. We want them to be good and useful men and women . . . we would point them forward and onward, saying as we do so, "Fortiter! Ascende!"

Unfortunately the centennial celebrations did not mark the beginning of a bright new era for the school, but instead were the beginning of the end of its existence as a private academy, a victim of the changes moving with ever greater force through Flatbush.

The last successful principal of the Hall was Reverend Robert Grier Strong, son of Reverend Thomas M. Strong. Reverend Robert Strong was born in Flatbush. He was a graduate of Erasmus Hall, New York University, and the New Brunswick New Jersey Theological Seminary located at Rutgers University. His wife also had deep ties to Flatbush. She too had been a student at Erasmus. Her father Dr. John B. Zabriskie, her grandfather Jeremiah Lott, her great-grandfather Bateman Lloyd, her great-great-grandfather Jacob Lefferts, her brother Dr. J.L. Zabriskie, and her nephew Dr. J.B. Zabriskie Jr. all served as school trustees. After Reverend Strong served as minister of several different congregations, the family returned to Flatbush, and in 1884 he became principal of Erasmus Hall Academy.

Strong, asssisted by his deep ties to the community, was the last principal to run the school profitably. But even under Strong the writing foretelling the end was on the wall. The old Flatbush families that had built Erasmus Hall and supported it over the years were leaving. Ironically, Erasmus Hall prepared them to leave their farms and make the transition into an urban world of professions and business.

After the death of Reverend Strong in 1892 the school rapidly went into a sharp decline. Dr. R. Arrowsmith, a graduate of Columbia College who had done his postgraduate work at Berlin University in Germany, succeeded him. It appears that his tenure at Erasmus was not a happy one and he stayed less than a year. In a letter dated January 25, 1906 to Dr. W.B. Gunnison, who became principal of Erasmus after it became a public high school, Arrowsmith outlined the factors that had undermined the academy. In addition to a long list of expensive changes to be made, Arrowsmith believed that the death of Reverend Strong precipitated the near collapse of the school. In his view:

> In 1892 the Academy became so demoralized for the death of Mr. Strong had weakened the ties of personal and Church loyalty to the Academy; a new population to whom the traditions of the school meant nothing, was rapidly taking the place of the old families; while the growth of the public schools had to a large extent left no place of the type of education which the Academy had provided for many years

In March 1893 Mary Wheeler Hawley, a graduate of the Van Wagenen's Training School in New York City, replaced Dr. Arrowsmith as principal, serving in that post until 1896.

In 1895, shortly after Flatbush had become incorporated into the City of Brooklyn, the board of trustees confronted the question of Erasmus Hall's future. The 1890s had not been kind to the school. Its constant financial problems made it difficult to maintain the facilities. Beginning with the tenure of Dr. Arrowsmith, the main building of the school served as a boarding house, and the few enrolled day pupils were taught in three old-fashioned rooms. The library, once the school's pride and joy, was out-of-date. New equipment was needed for the laboratories. There was pressure to institute an athletic program and that too would need to be equipped. The student body had severely declined from its peak, and the stellar reputation that the school enjoyed in earlier years had diminished. It was no longer attracting students from other states or countries. Even if the board of trustees wanted to invest in renovating the school, it was doubtful that the community of Flatbush would have supported it. The old families had been subdividing their land and selling it to real-estate developers and moving away and Flatbush had become a suburb of a thriving city. New people were moving into the area and the City of Brooklyn was providing free public schools that offered a fine education.

The trustees concluded that Erasmus Hall could no longer be maintained as a private institution and decided to approach the Brooklyn Board of Education and offer it to them as a public high school. It was a difficult decision to make because the old Flatbush families that supported it for so long had deep attachments to their academy. It was the alma mater of generations of many families, including the trustees. Nevertheless, in the late spring of 1895 John Z. Lott offered the following resolution that was unanimously adopted:

> Resolved. That it is the opinion of the Board that it is for the interest of the Academy and of the Twenty-ninth Ward of the City of Brooklyn that the Academy should be placed under the care of the Board of Education of the City of Brooklyn.
>
> Therefore resolved. That the Board offer the grounds of the Academy to the Board of Education of the City of Brooklyn upon the following conditions, viz: In consideration of the gift of land the Board of Education are to erect and maintain upon said land a High School Building of the same character and grade as other High School Buildings in the City of Brooklyn.

A committee of John Z. Lott, Henry Sherrill, and Dr. Homer L. Bartlett was appointed to bring the matter before the Brooklyn Board of Education.

After the matter was brought before the board, it responded by appointing a committee of Messrs. Weir, McNulty, and Zabriskie to investigate the offer and make a recommendation. Dr. Zabriske of Flatbush, who had served as a trustee of Erasmus Hall for many years, had been appointed to the Brooklyn Board of Education in 1894 when the village of Flatbush was annexed by the City of Brooklyn. Dr. Zabriskie died before the committee's work could be completed and Richard Young replaced him in November 1895. The minutes of the board of education show that at a meeting on December 3, 1895 the board accepted the trustees' offer:

> Resolved that this Board does hereby determine and decide to accept the gift of Erasmus Hall and the grounds in the Twenty-ninth Ward, and to establish and maintain a high school thereon in accordance with the stipulations contained in the proposition of the Trustees thereof, dated July 10, 1895, and the Corporation Counsel is hereby requested to prepare the necessary papers to vest the title of said buildings and grounds in the Board of Education of the City of Brooklyn.

With that simple resolution the people of the City of Brooklyn were given a gift of property then valued at $150,000, the reserve fund of $4,634.12, and the school library of approximately 2,000 volumes. On September 14, 1896, opening day of school in Brooklyn, Erasmus Hall made its debut as a public high school.

With the delivery of the deed to Erasmus Hall Academy to the board of education, the trustees ended an era of Flatbush history. For almost 250 years Flatbush had been a rural farming village with a stable population. Throughout the nineteenth century, for Flatbush, the tension between tradition and change had been unrelenting. Erasmus Hall embodied both elements. On one hand it was a traditional school presided over by the town elite. On the other the stated mission of the school, which the trustees made every effort to fulfill, was to train well-rounded young men and women able to shoulder responsibility in the larger world. They exceeded their goal, creating a cadre of professional, modern-minded graduates who went on to take their places as lawyers, jurists, doctors, elected officials, educators, and clergy. This high-quality education ended up providing the strongest challenge to the traditional society. It was inevitable that change would triumph, and with the deeding away of the academy the patrician past—though benevolent and public-spirited—was replaced by a new, democratic social order. The school had taught its lessons well.

The Farms

From the mid-seventeenth century well into the late nineteenth century, the people in Flatbush remained rooted to their land. Most were farmers and their farms were fertile and productive. They grew rich and were able to maintain their strong economy until almost the end of the nineteenth century. Most of the farmers did not work their farms themselves since there was always a plentiful supply of cheap labor available. In the early years Kings County was the largest slave-holding area in the North. Marc Linder and Lawrence S. Zacharias, authors of *Of Cabbages and Kings County: Agriculture and the Formation of Modern Brooklyn*, point out that at the end of the eighteenth century, fifty percent of the households in Kings County owned slaves and that ratio rose to two-thirds and three-fourths of the households, respectively, in Flatbush and New Utrecht. According to Linder and Zacharias:

> these extraordinary shares, which exceeded those of major slaveholding states such as South Carolina, were correlated with the predominance of the Dutch, who wanted slaves not as servants but as agricultural laborers as they sought to profit from feeding the metropolis.

Although more households owned slaves in Kings County than in the south, there were fewer slaves per household, and in Kings County slaves were given more freedoms (see chapter one). The largest slaveholders in the county in 1790 were Johannes Lott of Flatbush and Lawrence Voohries of New Utrecht; they held sixteen slaves each. In 1827 the New York state legislature outlawed slavery; however, as an institution, because of various exceptions in the law, slavery did not die out until the 1840s.

In the early days grains made up a large part of the Flatbush farm produce. However, after the opening of the Erie Canal in 1825, which allowed western grains to compete, the farmers of Kings County took advantage of their proximity to the cities of Brooklyn and New York and began growing perishable fruit and vegetables that had to be delivered daily. This produce was in great demand in these densely populated communities. As late as 1879 Kings County was only second to neighboring Queens County in the production and profitability of market garden products.

The Changing Landscape

After the Revolution and the British occupation ended, the town of Brooklyn industrialized and grew rapidly. By 1834 it had become a city and by mid-century it had grown to into the third largest city in the United States. At the same time the towns to its south (including Flatbush), initially shielded by the steep ridge of the terminal moraine, perhaps wishfully tried to hold onto their rural ways. Nevertheless, by mid-century they could feel the pressure of Brooklyn pushing up against their borders. It was probably the fact that the land-owning farm families had long held their property and were deeply entrenched, allowing them to maintain their rural life as long as they did. But by the 1870s the reality of living on the border of two major cities was upon them as more and more signs of suburbanization became obvious. In *Of Cabbages and Kings County*, Linder and Zacharias make this comparison:

> Someone standing on the highest hill in Flatbush in the 1860s . . . would have taken in a "vista of the finest farmlands in America, almost treeless for 6 miles and beyond, in full view of the Atlantic Ocean. To the south lay the village of Flatbush with its one thoroughfare, [the]Brooklyn and Flatbush Turnpike [Flatbush Avenue], winding its way through the most magnificent growth of ornamental trees in a country, the dwellings of the comfortable Dutch owners peeping through an occasional opening in the trees, giving evidence of thrift and competency.

Then quoting the editor of the *Kings County Rural Gazette*, H.J. Egleston, who viewing that same scene about ten years later could still praise the rural beauty of Flatbush, yet there was a difference. Unlike the first observer, Egleston recognized that pushing over the ridge were "the palatial residences of the merchant princes of the cities" and their proximity was a sign of the future. In an editorial Egleston predicted:

> that hundreds of dwellings would be built for the thousands of new residents following in the wake of rapid transit. . . . Already does the far-seeing eye of the speculator in real estate cast its keen penetrating gaze upon this beautiful southern slope, and soon with ruthless hand, the golden king will sway his potential scepter over our rural district, and perhaps entice our own staid citizens into a participation of the spoils which may accrue in a more full development of the advantages our village possesses as a place of abode.

In order to trace the changes in land use that took place in Flatbush between the end of the Revolution and the beginning of the twentieth century, three maps will be used. The first is a map showing the location of Flatbush's most prominent families in 1790. This map, which was probably constructed at a later date, lacks detail. Nevertheless, when compared with the map that has been most authenticated and well documented, Reverend Thomas Strong's 1842 map showing all the families of Flatbush, the 1790 map may be judged to be reasonably accurate. The origins of the third map, dated 1873, are unknown, although one can speculate that it was a real-estate map. It is perhaps the least trustworthy. However, it does show Flatbush in the early stages of transition from a rural to urban community. On this map, the beginning of the city street grid is visible, although all the streets had not been opened. (See pages 82–83)

Following the 1790 map from south to north: At the far southern end of the town, on the west side of Flatbush Avenue, (then known as the Flatbush Road or Main Street), in the area known as Little Flats, stood the house of William Allegeo (b. 1766). Allegeo, a cabinet maker by trade, was born in Montreal of English parents and moved to Flatbush after marrying the daughter of Vincintius Antonides. Her parents' home was on the opposite side of Flatbush Avenue. Vincintius Antonides was a descendant of the Reverend Antonides, who had been sent by the Classis of Amsterdam to preach at the Flatbush Church in 1704. In 1842 the grandson of William Allegeo, William Henry Allegeo, lived in his grandfather's house. In 1880 Gertrude Vanderbilt regretted that the family name of Antonides would end in Flatbush with the death of J. Antonides, who then occupied the family home. He was without a male heir.

A later addition to this area, shown on Dr. Stong's 1842 map, was the home of David Johnson that was adjacent to the farm of his father-in-law Mr. Parmalee (also not shown on the 1790 map). After Mr. Parmalee's death his property changed hands several times. In 1868 Newkirk Avenue, an east-west street that ran west from Flatbush Avenue to the Coney Island Road (now Coney Island Avenue), was opened. When Mr. Johnson died his widow sold the property and moved to Brooklyn. By 1880 a Mr. Giroux, the president of the Lafayette Insurance Company, owned the house. He and Charles Baxter of Brooklyn, who in 1870 built a house at the corner of Newkirk and Flatbush Avenues, were among the first of a new wave of "suburbanites," people who saw Flatbush as a "bedroom" community to the cities of Brooklyn and New York.

The next properties on the 1790 map were two farms, the most southerly belonging to Henry Ditmas and the next one to his brother John Ditmas. Ditmas was an old Flatbush family, the descendants of Jan Jansen, from Ditmarsum in the Duchy of Holstein in Holland. Jansen is said to have settled in Flatbush around 1647. Gertrude Lefferts Vanderbilt speculates that the houses were built before 1800 because, in spite of some alterations, they retained many of the characteristics of earlier Dutch architecture.

North of the Ditmas farms, the next house on Flatbush Avenue was the property of Judge Johnnes E. Lott (1746–1811) of the very large and prominent Lott Family of Flatbush and Flatlands. In 1769 Lott's father purchased this land from Daniel Polhemus, the son of Reverend Polhemus (the first minister of the Flatbush Dutch

Reform Church). Lott was one of six delegates elected to represent Kings County in the Provincial Congress held in New York City in 1776. Several years later, in 1784, he was appointed the first surrogate judge of Kings County, and later he became the first judge of the court. One of his sons, Jeremiah Lott (1776–1861), inherited the farm. Jeremiah was the only surveyor in Kings County and the chronicler of the Lott family. During the War of 1812 he was commissioned a captain in the Flatbush militia and served at Fort Greene, Brooklyn. On his return to civilian life, he served several terms in the New York State Assembly and, following in his father's footsteps, was appointed surrogate, a position he held for nineteen years.

Opposite the Lott home on the north side of Little Lane at Flatbush Avenue was the farm of Teunis Bergen. The small landmarked neighborhood of Albemarle-Kenmore Terrace, built between 1916 and 1918 as garden mews, is located on East 21st between Church Avenue and Albemarle Road, partly on land that was once a segment of the Bergen farm and partly on land once owned by the church. The next two houses south of the Bergen house belonged to the Schoonmaker family. The 1790s map indicates that Dr. John H. Livingston, the first principal of Erasmus Hall Academy, resided in one of these houses while he lived in Flatbush. On the 1842 map Dr. Adrian Vanderveer is shown as the owner of the more southerly of the two houses. Vanderveer later sold this house to Henry Lyles Jr., who had married the only daughter of Samuel G. Lott. Lyles (president of one of the largest savings banks in New York), tore down the old house and replaced it with a larger house. Dr. Vanderveer moved to the east side of Flatbush Avenue and built himself a house on Vernon Avenue that included a greenhouse and vineyard where he practiced horticulture and arboriculture.

The David Clarkson house, next door to the Schoonmakers, was originally built by the Reverend Bernardus Freeman, who purchased seven acres of land near the church. His only child, Anna Margaretta, married David Clarkson, her cousin, and probably inherited the house from her mother. During the Revolution this house was badly vandalized by Hessian troops who in a drunken orgy drank Clarkson's rare wines (see chapter two). The house, which by 1880 had been sold to J.C. Bergen, was according to Vanderbilt one of the oldest in Flatbush. She describes it as having "the low ceilings and the heavy cross-beams characteristic of the houses built by the early settlers." And she comments, "probably few [houses] have been left so entirely free from modern improvements. The heirs of Mr. J.C. Bergen have had the good taste to leave the house as it was built without attempting to modernize it."

The Clarkson family, after one of the sons married the daughter of Judge Vanderbilt, moved to land north of the church, settling in the area that is now East 21st Street and Caton Avenue. Caton Avenue, which opened in 1786, ran east-west from Flatbush Avenue to the Coney Island Road, and formed the boundary between the Clark and General Crooke farms. Today Clarkson Avenue and Crooke Place are streets in the area named for these families.

Next to the original Clarkson house on the 1790 map was the courthouse lot. Until 1832, except for the few years between 1668 and 1686 when the British tried to establish the English town of Gravesend as the new county seat, Flatbush, because of the centrality of its location, had been the center of government. In 1686 the British moved the courts back to Flatbush and a new courthouse and jail were built. In 1692 the Court of Sessions for Kings County ordered each town to build "a good pair of stocks and a good pound [whipping post]." These were built and stood in front of the jail. It is not clear how long the whipping post and stocks remained and there seems to be no mention of them being torn down. However, since Vanderbilt, who gives no other information, was able to find an elderly man who remembered seeing them, it is safe to speculate that they may have existed into the early nineteenth century. According to Vanderbilt's informant:

> The tall post on one end was the whipping-post; from this extended a horizontal beam in which were semicircular excavations graded from larger to smaller circumferences, to fit larger or smaller limbs; the other half of this horizontal beam, rising upon a hinge when lowered in its place, fitted exactly over the lower half, and when fastened down, secured the prisoners' legs in the rings thus formed.

In the winter of 1758 a fire burned either the jail or the courthouse to the ground. The townspeople were able to partially save the other building by pelting it with snowballs. Nevertheless, the remaining building had been badly damaged and was torn down; a new courthouse and jail were built.

The new building was larger. It had two stories in order to accommodate both the jail on the lower floor and the court above it. During the Revolution the British soldiers took the benches out of the courtroom and converted it to a ballroom. In 1792 it was decided that the court needed repairs, and since it was already too small a new courthouse was built. It was designed by James Robinson and was similar in design to the one that it replaced. It continued as the county court until 1832 when it too burned down.

As the population of Brooklyn exploded and Flatbush remained rural and sparsely populated, a conflict developed between the two towns over the location of the courthouse. Every weekday morning the stagecoach brought many people from Brooklyn who had business with the court. The stagecoach would stop at the Schoonmaker Inn, one of the taverns that were located on Flatbush Avenue near the courthouse. It was said that Alexander Hamilton and Aaron Burr were sometimes seen "arm and arm" entering the courthouse on behalf of clients. Although Flatbush notables fought to keep the court, many of the townspeople were ambivalent toward those daily visitors. On one hand they brought commerce to the town, while on the other, it was felt, their presence intruded on the community's rural tranquility.

Even before the fire in 1832, Brooklyn had been winning the battle for the courthouse. An editorial in the March 3, 1825 edition of *The Long Island Patriot*, a weekly newspaper published in Brooklyn, made a strong case for relocating the court to Brooklyn, stating in part:

> A remonstrance against the removal of the court-house has been circulated in the county, in which it is stated that Flatbush is nearer the center of the county. The fact we admit; but we think the center of population of infinitely more importance than the center of territory—it being the people who attend court, and not the acres of land; and that in a county extending but eleven miles the center can be of little importance.

In 1826 the state legislature gave legitimacy to Brooklyn's claims when it ordered that the Courts of Common Pleas and General Sessions of the Peace meet alternately in Brooklyn at the Apprentices' Library (the predecessor of the Brooklyn Museum of Art) and the court in Flatbush. In its 1829–1830 session the state legislature allowed Brooklyn to raise taxes in order to build its own courthouse. After the Flatbush courthouse and jail burned in 1832, a law was passed locating the court in Brooklyn. Although some of the tavern owners tried to maintain their establishments, with the removal of the courthouse and the business it brought, the land slowly reverted back to residential use.

Judge John A. Lott (1806–1878) purchased the courthouse land and the 1842 map shows that he built his home there. He is an important figure in the transition of Flatbush from a farming community to a comfortable middle-class suburb of the city. As a member of one of the most prominent Flatbush families he spent his career not as a farmer but as an accomplished attorney, man of affairs, and public servant.

Judge Lott graduated from the Erasmus Hall Academy, where he later became a trustee, and from Union College with honors. He then studied law with Henry E. Warner, Esquire, a distinguished New York City attorney. After practicing law briefly in Manhattan he transferred his offices to Brooklyn and formed a successful partnership with Henry C. Murphy (who later in life would be instrumental in building the Brooklyn Bridge) and Judge John Vanderbilt, his Flatbush neighbor. The law firm of Lott, Murphy and Vanderbilt achieved a national reputation for excellence and was influential in New York state affairs. In 1838 Lott was elected county judge, an office he held for four years. In 1842 he was elected to the state senate, where he served for four years before returning to his law practice. During his lifetime Lott served as a director or officer of many corporations, including the Flatbush Gas Company, the Long Island Safe Deposit Company, the Atlantic Bank of Brooklyn, and the Flatbush and Coney Island Railroad, of which he was president during its construction. That railroad, although begun as an excursion railroad to the Atlantic shore beaches at Brighton, Manhattan Beach, and Coney Island, was an important factor in the urbanization of Flatbush.

At the corner of Church Lane (also known as the Road to New Utrecht and Bath), now Church Avenue, stood the Reformed Dutch Church. The church, which still has an active congregation, is the oldest site of continuous religious practice on Long Island. The continuation of Church Lane on the east side of Flatbush was first called Cow Lane, and then East Broadway. That street is now Church Avenue, and the intersection of Church and Flatbush Avenues, at the center of Brooklyn, is one of the borough's best known crossroads.

North of Church Avenue, located south to north along Flatbush on the 1790 map, were the homes of Peter Lefferts, Senator John Vanderbilt, George Martense, Judge Martense, Leffert Lefferts, and Judge Vanderbilt. The Martense family were the descendants of Adrian Reyerse (d. 1710) of Amsterdam, who immigrated to Flatbush in 1646. He married Annetje, a daughter of Martin Roelofse Schenck of Flatlands. Their son, Martin Adriance (1668–1754), better known as Martin de Boer or Martin the Farmer, became the largest landholder in Flatbush. His farm stood on what is now the Parade Grounds (a large open area of twenty ball fields and a playground, opposite the south end of Prospect Park) and extended into New Utrecht. When he died the farm was divided into three: the north, south, and west farms, each of which was bequeathed to one of his sons, Rem (b. 1695), Garret (b. 1698), and Adrian (b. 1707). By Dutch custom, they reversed the name of their father and were called Martense or Martin's sons. Martense, in accordance with English custom, became the surname.

Although divided, and often leased to tenant farmers, the land stayed within the Martense family for several generations until the last quarter of the nineteenth century. Charles Andrew Ditmas, a scion of the Ditmas family, in his book *Historic Homesteads of Kings County*, with some bitterness blames the 1889 sale of some of the property of George Martense (the land originally left to Rem) as the beginning of the end of rural Flatbush. According to Ditmas:

> On February 20, 1889, Gertrude Prince, wifte of John Duffield Prince and daughter of George Martense, deceased; Mary Martense Prince, wife of John D. Prince, Jr. and daughter of Jacob V.B. Martense, deceased; Eliza Ann Martense, widow of Jacob Van Brunt Martense and Adrian Vanderveer Martense, their son and Helen Martense, their daughter, sold the old Martense Homestead, which for many years had been occupied by tenants. It was an historic sale, and was the beginning of the great real estate movement which was to culminate in the high prices of to-day and of still higher prices of the future. The purchaser was William Ziegler, and today the last semblance of farm life is being removed from this rural section. Within a stones throw from this house are row after row of one and two family brick houses. Only a short distance from three [trolley] car lines, this centrally located property abounds with interest to the speculators, who have had the good taste to call the section by the old and honorable name of Martense.

One of the last of the Martense family to carry the name was Rachel Martense (1801–1905), who lived to be the oldest person in Flatbush. The gossip was she had never married because of a sad love affair in her youth. She was a generous and compassionate woman who was in her later years called "Aunt Rachel." It is said that even when she was nearly one hundred and had failing eyesight she still sewed garments for the poor. After Rachel's death the land was sold to settle her estate and the estates of her brother-in-law, Captain William H. Story, who was married to her sister Maria and her nephew, Joseph S. Story, who had lived with her for many years.

Flatbush

The ancestor of the Lefferts family was Lefferts Pietersen Van Hagewout (d. 1704), who settled in Flatbush in 1660. Peter Stuyvesant gave him the deed to his farm, which remained in the family for eight generations, or about 250 years. The Lefferts family owned land on both the east and west sides of Flatbush Avenue, although the original homestead and the largest parcel was located on the east side. The house, Lefferts Manor or Lefferts homestead as it is now known, was rebuilt after the Revolution. It stood at 563 Flatbush Avenue until 1918 when it was moved to Prospect Park where it now stands (see chapter one).

One of the unusual features of the farm was a pond known as the Steinbokkery that in the early days was the subject of various ghost stories and superstition. The pond, which was located near today's Bedford Avenue, was about two acres in size. According to *Rambles About Historic Brooklyn*, a pamphlet that introduces itself as "a collection of the facts, legends, traditions and reminiscences that time has gathered about the historic homesteads and landmarks of Brooklyn," there were many Indian legends relating to the pond to which some of the settlers also subscribed:

> The Algonkins [*sic*], of whom the Flatbush Carnarsies were a sub-tribe believed that springs, brooks and ponds were gifts of the Great Spirit, hence sacred. . . . One [settler] Joris Van Nyse asserted that the Steinbokkery was a breeding place for sea-serpents and ghosts, and he further declared that one night when he was returning home from Ben Nelson's in Flatbush, on Clove Road near the Bridge, he saw four or five great serpents come out of the pond, their heads blazing flame, and that they followed the creek toward the ocean.

Rambles further reports that about the time Van Nyse said he saw the serpents and John Lefferts admitted to seeing "phosphorescent lights rising from the swamp and marshes," that he (Lefferts) and his neighbors had thought nothing of it. Raising a class distinction, Rambles concludes:

> The country folk were the ones who saw visions and wove tales of a supernatural nature about old Steinbokkery, interpreting what they saw as forerunners of some great calamity. The Indians in their turn believed that the pond was the home of fire dragons and that these monsters flew from one pond to another.

It is probably no coincidence that this is the same area where, according to early Dutch Legend, the devil danced and the old Domine met an apparition as he traveled home from Brooklyn (see chapter one).

It would appear from the early records that Lefferts was a very successful farmer. In 1676 they show that his holdings in stock and land were worth £104. By 1683 they had increased to £174/10. Beginning with his son Pieter (1680–1774), who served as county treasurer from 1737 to 1772, many members of the Lefferts family played prominent roles in the affairs of the town and county. Peter's son Jan Lefferts (1719–1776) held several public positions. He served as a judge on the Court of Sessions and Common Pleas, was the county clerk of Flatbush from 1773 to 1776, and was elected delegate to the Provincial Congress. His son Peter (1753–1791) was a state senator and also served as a judge. He was also a trustee of the Reformed Protestant Church and a major contributor to the building fund of Erasmus Hall Academy. He was also a staunch patriot and a lieutenant in the Flatbush militia. It was his house that was burned down by the Americans because the British were firing at them from behind it. The house was rebuilt after the war and now stands in Prospect Park (see chapter one).

Following in his family's footsteps, John Lefferts (1785–1829) spent much of his life in public service, first as county treasurer from 1811 to 1813, and then as a member of Congress from 1813 to 1821 when he was elected a state senator, an office he held from 1821 to 1826. In 1823 Senator Lefferts married Maria Lott. Their first child was Gertrude (1824–1902), the author of *A Social History of Flatbush*. Their second child was John 1826–1893), born two years later. In 1846 Gertrude married Judge John Vanderbilt (1819–1877). Charles Andrew Ditmas says of her: "Her life was largely spent in charitable pursuits. She was the author of an interesting book entitled *Social History of Flatbush*, and respected by all who knew her for her nobleness of mind."

Rambles tells this story concerning John (Gertrude's younger brother) who, like his sister, was well respected and loved by the town. The story describes John Lefferts as a tall (six feet four inches), powerfully built man who was generally good natured, courteous, and generous. However, he would not allow himself to be trifled with. One day, so the story goes:

> a donkey domesticated in his family for the pleasure of his children refused to go into an adjoining pasture. No persuasion could persuade him to move an inch. Mr. Lefferts wasted no time expostulating with the reluctant beast, but seized him by the tail and nape of the neck and threw him bodily into the adjoining field.

Some time after 1842 John Lefferts sold some lots on the southwest corner of the farm to Jeromus J. Johns, who built a freestanding house of Milwaukee brick. That property was sold several times until it was purchased in 1879 by Dr. Barlett, a physician, and his wife Margaret S. Bartlett, who was Dr. Strong's niece. When the street in front of the house was opened Mrs. Bartlett, who like Dr. Strong had been born in Cooperstown, New York, named it Fenimore Street after the great American writer and close friend of her father, James Fenimore Cooper.

On Dr. Strong's map, the home of Dr. Zabriskie's was the first house on the north side of Church Lane at the corner of Flatbush Avenue, on what was once part of a Lefferts farm. The Zabriskie family, through Abby Lloyd Zabriskie, were lineal Lefferts descendants. The house, which was torn down in 1877, was one of the old landmarks that according to Vanderbilt was:

> built so early that nobody could remember the time when and by whom it was built. In its heavy sloping roof, its long, narrow front stoop, and the low ceilings of its roomy first floor, it showed the characteristics of the houses which were built at an early period.

At the time of the Revolution, before the Zabriskie family occupied the house, it was the home of Jacob Lefferts. Lefferts, who had Tory leanings, was responsible for feeding a young American officer, Bateman Lloyd, who was a British prisoner on parole in Flatbush. It did not take long for the young officer and Lefferts's beautiful daughter Abigail to fall in love. Their love story is told in *Rambles*:

> How the love affair would have progressed, had it not been for an uncle of Abigail's who had no Tory scruples, cannot be surmised. It is safe to assume that the youthful prisoner broke his parole, and that most of his courtship was done at the home of the young woman's uncle, Mr. Jacobus Vandeventer. She left home one afternoon ostensibly to call on her relative, whose home was near what is now Mount Vernon Avenue [Vernon Ave on the map and presently Tilden Avenue] and the main street (Flatbush Avenue). A clergyman happened there at the same time, also Mr. Bateman Lloyd. The following morning Mr. Vandeventer appeared at the home of Mr. Jacob Lefferts on the corner of what is now Flatbush and Church Avenues, then known as the cross-roads.
>
> "Is Abby at your house?" asked Mr. Lefferts.
>
> "Yes, and her husband also," was the unexpected response. "Now, now," he may have continued, on seeing the wrath flame up in the good Tory's face, "better allow them to go in peace."
>
> The family was soon reconciled, the young couple given a paternal blessing, and Mr. Jacob Lefferts and his son-in-law became fast friends for life.

Jacob Lefferts willed the house to his son-in-law Bateman and his daughter Abigail. It was later passed to Dr. John Zabriskie, through his wife Abby Lloyd Zabriskie, daughter of Bateman and Abigail Lloyd. Dr. Zabriskie was a physician and a trustee of Erasmus Academy. He enjoyed reading and had built himself a fine library. In order to instill the love of reading in young people, he readily lent books from his library and enjoyed working on reading programs with the youth of the town.

Vanderbilt remembers how Mrs. Zabriskie's grandmother, Mrs. Lloyd, always sat at a window of the house that overlooked a large linden tree. Mrs. Lloyd, who lived to be past eighty would read and knit, and when she wanted to change her routine she cut pictures of fruit and foliage from periodicals and gave them to school children who always greeted her when they passed by. Vanderbilt still had one of the cutouts, "a neatly outlined tracery of twining leaves and branches, [that was] pasted upon one of the leaves of the old linden tree which shaded her window. The motto upon it read:—'We all do fade as a leaf,' It was dated 1839." At the time she made the cutout, Mrs. Lloyd was eighty-three years old. Commenting on the subtle allusions of the motto, Vanderbilt noted, "the passing years have in their changes seen the old lady borne to her grave, the tree fall from age, and the house in which she lived leveled to the ground."

That Linden tree, at an earlier time, was the setting of an often told story of a poignant meeting between three brothers. At that meeting, which took place during the Revolution, Major Lenox, an American patriot who was a British prisoner kept under parole in Flatbush, spoke with his brothers who were British sympathizers. His brothers had come to beg him to renounce the American cause. To which Major Lenox, with tears in his eyes, is said to have replied, "I will never do it."

One of the five great Linden trees of Flatbush, the tree stood on Church Lane near Flatbush Avenue. In the days before the Revolution it shaded General Washington and in the siege that followed, British officers enjoyed its shade as well. After the war it is said that iterant preachers held Sunday afternoon services under it. According to Vanderbilt, this tree was quite remarkable:

> An old English linden, it stood erect until the centennial celebration of the freedom of which it had witnessed the dawn A dead or dying branch was the only sign it gave of capitulation to Time, the great conqueror, until the full century of freedom was completed; then upon a quiet day when there was scarcely a breeze to account for its fall, it slowly yielded to the power of decay, and as if its own consent, without the compulsory power of the external elements, it gave up its life and fell to the ground.

Of the other great Linden trees, three stood on Flatbush Avenue: one near the old courthouse opposite Erasmus Hall, one near the southeast corner of Flatbush Avenue where a Citibank branch now stands, and the third at the corner of Flatbush Avenue and Grant Street (now Snyder Avenue). The last tree was in front of the house of General Philip S. Crooke.

The most northern entry on the west side of Flatbush on the 1790 map is the farm of Judge Vanderbilt. The 1842 map indicates that some of the land had been sold and additional houses built, and the 1873 map includes Prospect Park, which was open by 1868. Gertrude Lefferts Vanderbilt noted:

> The pleasantest portion of the original Vanderbilt farm is now enclosed in Prospect Park. The highest point there was formerly known as Vanderbilt Hill. It commands a more extended view than any other spot in the Park. The hill next, on which is the carriage-drive or Concourse, was also a portion of the Vanderbilt farm.

The Vanderbilts were descendents of Jan Aertson Vanderbilt, or Jan Aerson, from the Bild or Bilt. This, according to chronicler T.C. Bergen, was a manor in the province of Friesland. However, Gertrude Lefferts Vanderbilt disputes this. According to her, "the family tradition, however, is to the effect that this ancestor came from the

Baltic"—Jan van de Belt having that signification. This is strengthened by the fact that his first wife, Anneken, whom he married February 6, 1650, was from Bergen, Norway. A deed dated 1661 and signed by Governor Peter Stuyvesant conveying the farm on which he lived to Jan vande Bilt, was still in the family's possession in 1882.

The Vanderbilts were a very public-spirited family and their name was associated with all the "good works" of Flatbush from the seventeenth century until Gertrude's death in 1902. Her husband John died in 1877 at age fifty-eight after suffering through a long illness. A long, praiseful obituary in the Brooklyn *Eagle* celebrated his life and life in the rural towns of Kings County:

> In a time when rights were unknown he was a Democrat; . . . in a time when shysters had not been evolved, and when pettifoggers were limited to a satirical stage or a sarcastic literature, he was a lawyer; in a time when gentlemen were as dominant in politics and scholars as dominant in council as they now are not, he was a scholar and a gentleman. His rapidity of public development, his activity in affairs, his not surpassed qualities of good-fellowship, the magnetism of his mind and manners, and the impressive appeal which he could address to the people, early made him and long kept him what he was fondly called "Kings County's Favorite Son," when that appellation was forcible by its rarity, significant in its meaning, and when it had not been vulgarized by its application to the politicians by profession and to the place-hunters by occupation.
>
> It will be well remembered by those familiar with Brooklyn organized politics and society that the better led, but less "organized," years of the local democracy, the law firm of Lott, Murphy & Vanderbilt, was as thorough political as it was an eminent legal power in this country. These three gentlemen named, of whom the youngest died first, brought into local politics the principles of statesmanship, and to civil service the habits of fidelity, independence and diligence, and a grade of culture, force, and knowledge that have made their public records a bright part of the history of their country, just as their private careers have been a most honorable segment of the social and intellectual history of their city.

North of the Vanderbilt land, Dr. Strong's 1842 map shows that the Willink family, wealthy latecomers to Flatbush, built their mansion inside the area that would later become Prospect Park. An entrance to Prospect Park, located at the junction of Flatbush and Ocean Avenues and Empire Boulevard (then Malborne Street), is known as the Willink gate.

Mrs. Willink and her sister Miss Ludlow were descendants of the Van Horn family, one of the old, very rich Manhattan Dutch families. The Van Horns would take summer vacations in Flatbush, and one of their daughters, who married a Mr. Ludlow, apparently retained such fond memories of the town for many years that later, as a widow, she returned with her own two daughters, one unmarried and one married to

Mr. Willink. Gertrude Lefferts Vanderbilt, who was fearless in her own domain as the historian of elite Flatbush, seemed a bit intimidated by the background of these new people who had their own pew at Trinity Church in Manhattan and traveled in the "first of circles" of New York Society. When Willink bought the property, Vanderbilt speculated that the old Mrs. Ludlow was delighted to have an opportunity to become reacquainted with her childhood friends. But to Vanderbilt's amazement, it turned out not to be the case:

> They [Mrs. Ludlow, her daughters and Willink] desired entire seclusion; except in business relations, they wished for no communication with the outer world. Whether it was merely a freak which became afterward a habit, no one could tell.
>
> The result, from whatever cause, was an entire withdrawal from society. No retreat could have been more closely guarded against the intrusion of visitors; whether acquaintance, friend, or relative tapped at the door, the rebuff was always given, and no one passed beyond the portal of that stately mansion after once the carpenters had left and the four elderly persons who comprised the family.
>
> The windows were never opened. The furniture, great crates of which stood in the parlors, was never unpacked. The silver service on which had been given the hospitable and stylish dinners of earlier times was consigned to a vault in the cellar. In the basement were kept great bull-dogs fed on raw meat, to guard the premises at night, for it was whispered about that they had such stores and hoard of silver.

Mr. Willink was vigorous but getting on in years. The son of a wealthy Holland banker, he had boasted that his family was long lived. Alas, it was not to be his fate. Mr. Willink's one indulgence was that he loved lively horses and took great pleasure in driving them around his estate. Then, according to Vanderbilt:

> They ran away with him one day. The vehicle in which he rode was entirely inclosed [*sic*] with glass in front, as if even when out on the street he would have something between himself and the outer world. He could not control his horses under this disadvantage. He was thrown out of his carriage and picked up dead on the road just before the house of his overseer.

After the death of their mother and Mr. Willink, the two sisters continued their seclusion, breaking it only occasionally to go to Trinity Church in Manhattan. Miss Ludlow, who Vanderbilt describes as a "tall, gaunt woman" who in her younger days would have been quite attractive had she "not rejected every thing that was tasteful in dress, and assumed the most austere and rigidly plain style of garments," managed the family affairs and estate. Vanderbilt thought she was a smart and shrewd businesswoman who husbanded the family fortune carefully, except for the eccentricity on occasion when they showed "unbounded generosity," often surprising a peddler by purchasing all his merchandise or giving most generously to a church charity.

To the town's surprise the sisters decided to build a hotel on some property they owned south of Church Lane. The sisters rented the hotel on very liberal terms to a hotelkeeper, but according to Vanderbilt, their constant interference in the business kept it from being a success.

The last sister to die was Miss Ludlow. Nobody attended her funeral. She was the last person in the family and she was interred in the family vault at Trinity Church. The house that had been so jealously closed, Vanderbilt continued, "was now thrown open to the inspection of the world." And what people saw was a house full of cobwebs, dust, and debris. The valuables and the junk were mixed together indiscriminately. Vanderbilt must have enjoyed this story, because she ends saying, "We make no apology for dwelling so long on this, one of the few romantic histories of our village, for had not every old town its bit of romance? And why should not such be recorded along with other annals?

Traveling back north to south on the east side of Flatbush Avenue, opposite Judge Vanderbilt's property, was the Hegeman farm. Next door was Melrose Hall, the home of Revolutionary War veteran Colonel Aquila Giles. At the end of the war Giles purchased Melrose Hall, the estate confiscated from the British sympathizer William Axtell. Ironically, during the war Giles had secretly courted and later married Axtell's niece Eliza Shipton, who had spent the war years in the house awaiting Giles's return.

Melrose Hall, or Melrose Abbey as it was also known, was considered one of the grandest houses in Flatbush. The house stood on twenty-eight acres of what had once been part of a Vanderbilt farm. The land had been sold to Frederick Lane, an Englishman, who in 1749 built the house and gardens. The main part of the house was two and a half stories tall, and had two one-story wings on either side. The house stood back from Flatbush Avenue, protected by a grove of pine trees. The English style architecture of the house was very different from all the other Flatbush houses. And the inside, with its oak paneled ballroom, library, and gilded cornices, was far too ornate for the thrifty Dutch farmers. Gertrude Lefferts Vanderbilt considered the house ostentatious:

> In 1749 he [Lane] built what was, for that age, a large and showy house; it had a greenhouse at the rear. The cornices in the drawing-rooms were gilded, the rooms wainscoted, and the halls wide. The grounds were laid out in flower-beds; beyond the garden was a handsome lawn; Mr. Lane was an Englishman of good family who was banished from his home on account of the wild life he led. He had married a woman of low parentage and they lived here on an annuity which ceased at his death; after that she could not support the style in which they had lived, and the house was offered for sale, and purchased by Colonel Axtell.

Over the years Melrose Hall, which had a reputation as being haunted, had more owners than any other house in Flatbush. During the Revolution the Tory traitor Colonel William Axtell entertained British officers and their prominent American supporters, while American prisoners were being held in a basement dungeon. Some considered the house haunted and human remains were in fact found on the premises, adding to its sinister aura. Vanderbilt notes however that the remains were probably of British soldiers who were known to have been buried there.

One of the later owners of the house was the well-known actress and writer Anna Cora Mowatt. In her autobiography she remembered Melrose Abbey as being "a very pleasant residence." Describing her life and home in Flatbush, Mowatt wrote:

> I was excessively fond of the country and early in the spring [1835] Mr. Mowatt took me to reside in Flatbush, Long Island. The house in which we boarded was a large old fashion mansin, built before the Revolution [1750] and belonged to General [Aquila] Giles. There were dark and spacious vaults beneath the kitchen, where it was said that English prisoners had been confined, and there was a secret chamber above the great ballroom, to which no access could be found, save by a small window. The neighbors affirmed that a young girl had been purposely starved to death in that chamber, and that her ghost wandered at night about the house. Indeed, this report had gained such credence that nothing could have induced many of the older inhabitants of the village to pass a night beneath the haunted roof. . . . I became so much attached to this place that Mr. Mowatt purchased it for my gratification; stipulating however, that I should content myself in passing the greater portion of the year in the country. I gladly consented. The house was repaired and refurnished; the gardens and orchards enlarged, and planted with innumerable variety of fruit trees and flowers. . . . We gave our place the name of Melrose, not from any likeness it bore to Melrose Abbey, but on account of the abundance of roses that filled our greenhouses and covered the grounds.

In 1844 Dr. John Robinson, a physician whose practice was in New York, purchased the property and lived there with his family until 1879 when he died. After his death the property was sold. Its final owner was Dr. Homer L. Bartlett, who bought it in 1883. Bartlett seemed to be a forerunner of the real estate developers who would soon descend upon Flatbush. He planned to build a residential development called Melrose Park on the estate grounds. To accomplish this he removed the two wings and moved the house from its location at Flatbush and Parkside Avenues further east to Bedford Avenue near Winthrop Street. His plan never succeeded and the truncated Melrose Hall was demolished in 1903.

Continuing south down the east side of Flatbush Avenue, Giles's neighbors, according to the 1790 map, were William B. Gifford, Philip Nagle, Garret Stryker, and Peter Stryker, whose house was close to the corner of Cow Lane (and later East

Broadway), the earliest names for Church Avenue. The Stryker family was one of the oldest in Flatbush. Their ancestor Jan Stryker came from the Netherland province of Drenthe in 1652; his son Peter became one of the pantentees on the patent issued by Governor Dongon. In 1840 Garret Stryker sold his house to Helen Martense, who eventually gave it to her son Jacob V.B. Martense, who occupied it in 1880. At the corner of Cow Lane and Flatbush, diagonally across from the church, stood the Liberty Pole. Along the north side of Cow Lane stood the Brewery, the Neefus Farm, and the Schenck Farm.

On the south side of Cow Lane, between it and the road to Canarsie or Canarsie Lane (today a distance of five or six long city blocks lined with stores), was in 1790 the location of the Village School, Erasmus Hall Academy, and Reverend Peter Lowe's house. South of Reverend Lowe's residence were the Hegeman and Van Beuren houses, and the Vanderventer house and farm. Other farms in the area included the Remsen, Kouwenhoven, and Stryker farms. The 1842 map shows that a new street, Vernon Avenue, now Tilden Avenue, had been opened south of East Broadway and north of the Road to Canarsie and that many changes had taken place on Flatbush Avenue, including the addition of new homes and a store.

Reverend Peter Lowe (1764–1818), whose house was located just to the south of the Erasmus Academy, was a former student of Dr. Livingston. He was called to the church in 1787. His co-minister, the Reverend Martinus Schoonmaker (1737–1824), had been called two years earlier in 1785 from his church in Gravesend. Schoonmaker purchased property and built his house on the west side of Flatbush Avenue. In 1842 his property was still occupied by his descendents. It was during the tenure of these two ministers, the last to serve the six unified Reformed Churches of Kings County, that a significant change was made in the service. In 1792 it was decided that afternoon services would be in English. Reverend Lowe conducted the English services and Reverend Schoonmaker, who never quite learned the English language, became the last minister to preach in Dutch.

The 1842 map shows changes to this area. A new house and store that had been built by Michael Schoonmaker in 1823 were still standing in 1880. The house became the parsonage for Reverend Strong (1797–1861), who accepted the call to the church in 1822. To the south of the parsonage was Erasmus Hall Academy.

The two chroniclers of nineteenth-century Flatbush, Reverend Thomas Morris Strong, who during the nearly forty years of his ministry had participated in all the town's public events and projects and ministered to almost all the families in their good times and bad, and Gertrude Lefferts Vanderbilt, who was born, raised, educated, and died in Flatbush, say very little about themselves. Nevertheless, it is through their literate writing, keen eye for detail, and intimate knowledge of the culture and the place that the town and its people are brought to life and a history of those lives exists. Gertrude Leffert's Vanderbilt in her book gave tribute:

> Dr. Strong was the pastor of this church for a period of thirty-nine years. As a minister he had the respect of the church; as a true friend he was beloved

> by his people; as a Christian gentleman he was remarked for his courteous manners and the quiet dignity of his deportment. In time of trouble he was ever ready with sympathy, and the cordiality with which he met those who sought him for pastoral instruction served to bind him to them in affectionate regard.

Mrs. Vanderbilt too was remembered as a prominent woman who did much charitable work and wrote a history of Flatbush. For example, *Flatbush Today*, a publication of the All Souls Church, recalled her as a historian of home and hearth:

> When ones thoughts are directed to the women of Old Dutch stock in Flatbush they infallibly lead, first of all, to these women's historian Mrs. Gertrude Lefferts Vanderbilt. It was this elderly lady, though not so elderly 28 years ago when she "took her pen in hand" and gave to the world what must always remain as the one complete account of the Flatbush home. The times have indeed changed. The Flatbush of today bears small resemblance to that which Mrs. Vanderbilt wrote, when she said: "At an early period all the families in this county were united through marriage and intermarriage, thus forming one large family circle."

From the perspective of the twenty-first century, it is unfortunate that the legacy of this gifted historian was not fully appreciated. And that the social mores of her time prevented a woman as accomplished as she from participating in an active institutional role by, for example, serving as a trustee of Erasmus Hall, as an elder of the church, or in any other public position. Mrs. Vanderbilt herself, however, may have not felt deprived. In 1900 she joined with other women from prominent New York families to speak out against giving women the right to vote.

Reverend Strong's book, *The History of Flatbush*, had its origin in a series of lectures he had prepared in the winter of 1841–1842 for the Literary Society of Flatbush. Urged to publish the lectures by people who had either heard or heard of them, Reverend Strong allowed their publication with some editorial changes. It was his stated goal to make the book as complete and accurate as he could. There were problems, however. Much of the town's early history was contained in church records written in Dutch. To make matters worse, Reverend Strong complained about the "very small and cramped character" of the penmanship. Fortunately, he was helped to decipher and translate several important documents by John C. Vanderveer and Jeremiah Lott, Esquire, whom the author thanks. These men also provided the draft of the 1842 map that has become a standard cartographic reference. In addition, Reverend Strong was able to talk to some of the elderly people who had been witnesses to the events during the Revolution and its aftermath. Nevertheless, he is still concerned about accuracy because of the paucity of records. While Reverend Strong was writing his manuscript, Romeyn Brodhead, Esquire, went to the Netherlands on behalf of the state of New York in order to retrieve documents relating to the settlement of New Netherlands.

Strong looked forward to the publication of those documents because he believed they would provide a complete history of Dutch rule. Today, the Holland Project, under the auspices of the New York State Library and the Holland Society of America, is translating and publishing the records and documents pertaining to that era.

In the introduction to her book *The Social History of Flatbush*, Gertrude Lefferts Vanderbilt acknowledged a twofold purpose. On one hand, in order to preserve the history and memory of the town, she continued the story of Flatbush Reverend Strong had begun by documenting the changes that had taken place. "The day is probably not far distant," she wrote, "when [Flatbush] will become a part of the adjoining city of Brooklyn; then all traces of its village life and its individuality as a Dutch settlement will be lost." On the other hand, however, she intended to tell the story from a different perspective:

> In all love and respect for the memory of Dr. Strong, I have taken up the pen which he laid down, not so much in continuation of his subject as to give it from a different standpoint. As a woman, I have inclined to the social side of life and have endeavored to record the changes which time has made among the people in their homes and the fireside.

Continuing south along the east side of Flatbush Avenue: In 1871 one finds that a new Chapel of the Church was completed. It stood south of East Broadway, on the corner of Flatbush Avenue and the newly opened Grant Street (now Snyder Avenue) on the site previously occupied by the house of J. Vanderveer and a blacksmith shop. The chapel was used as a Sunday school room and for prayer meetings. A few years later, in 1875, the Flatbush Town Hall was built further east on Grant Street (35 Snyder Avenue), near the corner of what is now Bedford Avenue. Some years before the new town hall was opened, Richard L. Schoonmaker built a two-story addition to the store. The second floor of that building was used as a public hall, known as Schoonmaker Hall. After the town hall became the venue for public meetings Schoonmaker Hall was rented as a lodge to the Freemasons of Flatbush.

Grant Street also led to what the town called the "English Neighborhood." As Flatbush grew, the old ethos of total self-sufficiency gave way to hired mechanics. To house this non-farm population, a new section of town called "the English Neighborhood" was established. In this area the land was subdivided into small lots to provide housing for the mechanics and their families.

South of Canarsie Lane, on the east side of Flatbush Avenue on both the 1790 and 1842 maps, are the adjoining farms of the brothers Garret and John C. Vanderveer, who were quite elderly in 1842. The Vanderveer family, descendents of Janse Vanderveer, who came to New Netherlands in 1669 from Alkmaar, a free city on the North Holland Canal, were among the oldest in Flatbush. In 1880 descendants of the Vanderveer brothers were still living on the farms.

A huge windmill was located on the farm until 1879, when it burnt to the ground. Windmills were a common sight in Holland but a rarity in Flatbush. This windmill had special significance because it had been used to shelter the black population during the 1863 Civil War draft riots that had spread from New York to Brooklyn.

Although fires were a major problem in the densely built cities of Brooklyn and New York, they were less so in the more sparsely populated rural towns where there was still enough space between the buildings. The Vanderveer mill fire, however, was rare and apparently so spectacular that Vanderbilt reprinted a newspaper story about it:

> Last Tuesday night [March 4, 1879] about a quarter before seven o'clock, a fire broke out in the Vanderveer Mill, on the farm of Messrs. John Vanderveer & Sons, between Canarsie Lane and Pardaegat Pond. The spectacle of its destruction was such as has rarely been witnessed, and, mingled with the many people of the town who had gathered, were those who had been attracted for miles by the flames which lit the sky. The strong oak timbers stood up until the very last, while the shingles which covered it fell away, sending showers of sparks, which against the sky looked like gold-dust sprinkled on a cloth of blue. Still the flames burned on till nothing remained but the bare timbers raising gaunt arms appealingly against destruction; but the element did its work, and after a couple of hours had passed, that which it had taken years to build, and which had stood time's ravages for three quarters of a century, was laid in ruins.
>
> It was the first windmill erected on Long Island. It was completed in 1804, having begun about three years before by John C. Vanderveer, father of the present owner. It was of immense strength, the main timbers being 28 feet high and 2 and a half feet thick, hewn from trees grown on the farm. The carpenter was Abijah Baldwin, Joseph Mead being the millwright. John Oakely Sr., father of the present assistant district attorney, worked on it as an apprentice. It was four stories high, with a stone foundation of about 3 feet. The arms and sails were 26 feet long. The sails were first blown off in the famous September gale of 1821, and repaired by Baldwin. About ten years after the sails were again blown off, since which time they have not been repaired, the building was being used as a storehouse for hay, etc. It was full at the time of the fire. When it was working, farmers came from the adjoining counties with their grist for the famous mill. The view from the upper windows was very fine, and included Coney Island, the Narrows, Jersey, and Rockaway, and all places within a radius of 20 miles. During the draft riots of 1863 it was a refuge for African Americans of the village, where they held it in grateful remembrance.

Breaching the Final Barrier

The rocky ridge that was the southern terminus of the final glacier of the last ice age had for centuries been a natural barrier separating the town of Brooklyn and the towns to its south. During the Revolution it could only be crossed through four passes and the Shore Road. At the end of the war the town of Brooklyn, which was situated on the harbor and included Gowanus, turned its back on the rocky barrier and faced forward toward New York. It grew rapidly, using its harbor resources to build a commercial and industrial base, and by absorbing new population from the large influx of immigrants who began arriving in the 1840s. By the 1850s Brooklyn was the third largest city in the United States with a population of 96,838. By 1870 that population had grown to 266,661 and it was pushing at its southern borders.

The differences between Brooklyn and the towns to its south, including Flatbush, grew. As Brooklyn made itself into a city, the towns used the ridge as a shield in order to protect their rural character. Early in the nineteenth century the Flatbush community seemed to have thought it could succeed in holding back time. But the needs of Brooklyn's burgeoning population for space put severe pressure on agriculture. Farming in an area next to an expanding city increasingly became an inefficient use of valuable land.

By the 1870s the New York State legislature, reacting mostly to pressures from Brooklyn, decided the solution to the land problem was to annex Flatbush and the other towns to the City of Brooklyn. In 1873 it formed a commission of representatives of each town to "devise a general plan," to effectuate annexation to the City of Brooklyn. Judge John A. Lott, as one of Flatbush's most prominent lawyers and richest landholders, represented the town. He was also elected chairman of the commission. Lott was a strong supporter of annexation, believing that the future was in consolidation. He and other members of the Flatbush elite had already begun to diversify their interests. His major interlocutor was Teunis G. Bergen of New Utrecht, who was related to Teunis Bergen of Flatbush. Bergen was vehemently against any form of annexation. The question of consolidation brought to a head the tensions between those who wanted to maintain their rural setting and those who were ready for change. The underlying issue was lifestyle. The debate, however, was framed around the issue of taxation. Even after the Brooklyn representatives agreed that agricultural lands would be taxed at a lesser rate, the farmers were not ready to concede that they needed any additional government services and they were unwilling to pay. Since the veto over annexation was held in the towns—a majority of the voters of all the agricultural towns had to agree to it—the plan went down to defeat.

Those who opposed annexation won the day handily. This brought Flatbush and the other rural towns a measure of respite, albeit temporary. To celebrate its continued independence the town decided to build a new town hall to serve as a government facility housing the mayor's office, police department, criminal court, and jail. Yet even as the building was grandly opened in 1875, it was widely recognized by the townspeople that Flatbush would not be able to escape the incursion of the city much longer. At least two of the richest and most powerful families, the Lotts and the Lefferts, had favored annexation in 1873. At that time those families and others had already begun the process of shifting their personal fortunes from an economy based on agriculture and land to the more fluid monetary economy afforded by the professions, particularly law and business.

The inevitable happened in 1894 when Flatbush, Gravesend, and New Utrecht were incorporated into Brooklyn, joining the formerly independent towns of Williamsburg,

Bushwick, and New Lots, which had been annexed earlier. When New Lots opted for annexation in 1886, it had already become the second most populous town of Kings County. Thirty-four years earlier, in 1852, New Lots, which had been founded by Dutch farmers seeking more land for their children, separated from Flatbush. At the time of its annexation, in addition to the farm enclave, three urbanized towns, Brownsville, Cyprus Hills, and East New York had developed there. In 1895 with the annexation of Flatlands, the last holdout, the City of Brooklyn became conterminous with Kings County. On January 1, 1898, the City of Brooklyn became the Borough of Brooklyn, one of the five boroughs of the consolidated City of Greater New York. By the early 1900s, after 250 years of rural life, real estate developers were rapidly turning Flatbush into a suburb of the city, adapting it to the new urban environment of twentieth-century New York.

When contrasting a map of Flatbush in 1873 with the 1842 map published by Reverend Strong, the most salient features of the 1873 map were all the new streets. Forecasting the future, that map already showed a city grid carved out of farmland being rapidly filled with new houses. Most of the people who moved to Flatbush's new residential sections were escaping the dirt and grime of the cities. They clearly were not engaged in agriculture, and since the Flatbush economy was still agrarian-based, these newcomers probably worked in either the City of Brooklyn or the City of New York. They were the wave of the future—suburban commuters. Even before it was completed in 1874, Prospect Park was an important factor in spurring development south of the ridge.

Although it would soon change, on the 1790 map all the land north of Church Lane (now Church Avenue), almost to the border with Brooklyn, had been in the hands of three families: the Lefferts, Vanderbilts, and Martenses. These families and the Lott family formed the core of the social and political elite of the town. They had been the leadership that had pulled the town back from devastation after the Revolution, and with their championship of Erasmus Hall Academy revitalized the community. It was the loss of this traditional core that Gertrude Vanderbilt grieved. During the nineteenth century the farm town of Flatbush evolved from a land-based, self-sufficient entity into a suburb of Brooklyn. As Flatbush grew, these families lost the moral authority that land, kinship, and tradition had vested in them. At the same time families were shedding their traditional roles for two main reasons: first they recognized that their land was more valuable as real estate subdivision than as farm, and second with the improvements in education brought by Erasmus Hall Academy many were naturally moving away from the land into the professions and business where they emerged as leaders in the legal and business communities of Brooklyn and New York. After Flatbush was annexed by Brooklyn in 1894 and new taxes were put on the land, holding it became untenable.

The first area of population growth was on the east side of Flatbush Avenue, where many of the new streets were opened. From north to south the streets running east from Flatbush Avenue are Malbone Street (now Empire Boulevard, which forms the present border between the neighborhoods of Flatbush and Crown Heights), Sterling Street, Lefferts Avenue, and East New York Avenue (now Lincoln Road). Lincoln

Road is the northern boundary of one of the oldest Flatbush neighborhoods, Lefferts Manor. Lefferts Manor, built on part of the James Lefferts farm, is bounded on the east by Rogers Avenue, on the south by Fenimore Street, and on the west by Flatbush Avenue. Lefferts was one of the first members of an old settler family to recognize that his land was more valuable as a subdivision than as farmland. In 1894 he divided much of his farm into 600 lots that he sold to developers, with restrictions. These restrictions required that all houses in Lefferts Manor be one-family, cost at least $5,000 to build, be at least two stories high, and be built of either stone or brick. The other streets in Lefferts Manor are Maple Street, Midwood Street, and Rutland Road.

South of Fenimore Street are Hawthorne and Winthrop Streets, Diamond Street, (now Parkside Avenue) and Ridgewood Avenue (now Clarkson Avenue). Lenox Road was added to the grid later and located between Clarkson and Caton Avenues. The next street is Linden Boulevard, a major artery that runs east from Flatbush Avenue to Queens. Martense Street lies between Linden Boulevard and East Broadway (Church Avenue). The grid south of Church Avenue to Vernon Avenue (Tilden Avenue) was less developed, and more broken by small streets. South of Vernon Avenue the streets were developed at the turn of the century as more and more farms were subdivided and sold to the real estate developers who often developed whole communities. Those communities, several of which are now New York City Historic Districts, were developed mostly in the very early twentieth century and are now collectively known as the neighborhoods of Victorian Flatbush.

In the 1870s the grid was more spare on the west side of Flatbush Avenue. However, two major north to south through streets were opened in 1876. The first was Ocean Avenue, which began near the Willink gate to Prospect Park, at the junction of Flatbush Avenue and Empire Boulevard, and extended south as far as Manhattan Beach (on the Atlantic Ocean). Ocean Avenue was developed in the early years of the twentieth century when many high-rise apartment houses were built. The other important road was Ocean Parkway, a toll road designed by Prospect Park architects Frederic Law Olmsted and Calvert Vaux as a grand parkway from Prospect Park to Coney Island.

Prospect Park was opened in 1868 and completed in 1874. The idea for building a great park in Kings County came from the City of Brooklyn, which was engaged in building great public works and cultural institutions. Flatbush on the other hand continued well into the 1870s and 1880s to view itself as a rural village of self-sufficient farms, and with the exception of building Erasmus Hall Academy seemed to take no interest in building cultural institutions. Although the park was built on land located in both Flatbush and Brooklyn, Flatbush seemed almost indifferent to its development. Nevertheless, Flatbush could not escape the effect of the park on town life. Concomitant with its development, Flatbush Avenue was straightened, widened, and paved. Other new roads were added. These new roads, coupled with significant improvements in transportation including the early steam railroad, trolley cars, the subway, and finally the passenger car, changed Flatbush from a rural town into an urban neighborhood—the place that would be a suburb of Brooklyn.

Chapter Four

FLATBUSH IN THE TWENTIETH CENTURY

In what seemed like an instant—a brief thirty years—the patrician Flatbush of Gertrude Lefferts Vanderbilt vanished. The rapidity and thoroughness of its transformation was breathtaking. The large, well-kept farmhouses, with their neat picket fences that lined Flatbush Avenue were gone. In their place was a wall of storefronts, some with apartments above them. The quiet Main Street changed from a winding country road where cows once wandered into Flatbush Avenue, a busy commercial thoroughfare. Streetcars, trucks and automobiles soon replaced the horse drawn carts of the farmers. New residential neighborhoods stood where farms once had been. The old families that for 250 years presided benevolently over the town of Flatbush were gone, replaced almost entirely by new populations. And, the changes that later took place over the course of the twentieth century were just as stunning.

Between 1880 and 1910 powerful forces that had been pushing the margins of Brooklyn and New York outward during the nineteenth century coalesced. The strongest of the imperatives driving the expansion of the two cities—the great waves of European immigration (the first in 1840s and 1850s, the second between 1880 and 1924), the completion of the three East River Bridges (the Brooklyn Bridge in 1883, the Williamsburg Bridge in 1903, and the Manhattan Bridge in 1910), and the juggernaut industrialization of the cities of Brooklyn and New York—were beyond the control of Flatbush. Nevertheless, the consequences of each forever altered it.

Other, more immediate factors that changed Flatbush, but also remained beyond its control, were the need of Brooklyn's rapidly growing population for residential housing, the opening of Prospect Park in 1868, the sometimes resisted annexation of the town by the City of Brooklyn in 1894, and a concomitant increase in property taxes. Most important, however, were the new modes of transportation that eliminated barriers to large-scale population movement within Brooklyn and New York, enabling people to commute greater distances between home and work.

Finally, there were the actions taken by the town of Flatbush. First, the building of Erasmus Hall Academy provided the young with a quality education that enlarged their world view, prepared them for the professions, and reduced their interest in farming. Second, and perhaps most significant, the major landholding families were finally willing to sell their land to outside developers. For most of these families, who for years either rented their farms to tenants or ran them initially with slave and later with hired labor, the decision was also based on economics; the land had become too valuable for agriculture. To the credit of the sellers who sold on condition that the land be used for housing and the developers who adhered to those conditions and built new residential communities, Flatbush became one of the first suburbs of the city. Factories and other industrial facilities were not permitted. Even today the commercial areas serve the needs of local consumers—and there is no manufacturing or heavy industry.

Later, in the 1920s, 1930s, and post World War II, massive amounts of six-story high-rise apartment construction brought in thousands of new residents, immigrants, and their children fleeing the ghettos and slums of Manhattan and Brooklyn for a better life. Their raw energy created a very different Flatbush, full of startling contrasts between civil service, garment-industry workers, union organizers and construction workers, and the upper-income doctors, lawyers, engineers, and business owners.

Trains and Trolleys

The changes that would permanently transform Flatbush from a quiet farming village into a bustling suburb of a large city, which in turn was surrounded by densely populated high-rise apartment developments, began in earnest shortly after the Civil War with the opening of Prospect Park and the development of the Brooklyn-Flatbush and Coney Island Railroad. Although improved roads and the new modes of transportation were sufficient in and of themselves to make it possible for large populations to commute between work and home, the influence of Prospect Park, which opened in 1868 and was completed in 1874, cannot be overstated. The jewel landscape architects Frederick Law Olmsted (1822–1903) and Calvert Vaux (1824–1895) created at the center of Brooklyn dissolved the rocky ridge of the terminal moraine that had separated the towns of Flatbush and Brooklyn, and made Flatbush accessible to large populations. The park also suggested an urban aesthetic that was followed by the developers who opened the farmland to the south. The integration of nature into an increasingly urban lifestyle was duly noted by the publication *Flatbush of Today* (1908), a periodical of All Souls Universalist Church:

> Between the Flatbush of today and Brooklyn stands still the great ridge of hills which kept the tides of population from overflowing into the flatlands of the old Dutch farms. But Prospect Park has changed the hills from a place of gloom into the fairest pleasure ground the whole world has. Winding roads, enticing paths, vistas of meadows—green as the lawns of England, lakes with sinuous shores, brooks broken into noisy waterfalls, groves where art has adorned but not despoiled nature—the hand of man reverently keeping the old forests, but adding to them the grace of human art and taste.

Building the park entailed widening and straightening Flatbush Avenue, the park's eastern border, and building two great boulevards modeled on the Champs Elysees in Paris. The first, Eastern Parkway, ran east from the park along the ridge of the terminal moraine. The other, Ocean Parkway, extended from the southern boundary of the park to Coney Island. These elegant roads were intended to bring people to the park. And, although Ocean Parkway is a few blocks west of Coney Island Avenue, and therefore technically outside the boundaries of Flatbush, the additional access it provided added to the appeal of Flatbush as a suburb. By the early twentieth century it had become quite desirable for those who could afford it, to move their families into what was then thought of as "the realm of light and air"—the more healthy and open environment of Flatbush—and commute to their work in the city.

Writing in the publication *The Realm of Light and Air*, published by All Souls Universalist Church in 1905, Flatbush resident Mrs. Mary E. Craigie saw the area as a panacea—the ideal place to make a home and raise a family in the urban environment:

> The problem of the twentieth century is the problem of the family. How and where to establish in our great city a satisfactory home is the complex question many are trying to solve. How to provide a proper environment for children and how to secure reasonable seclusion and independence under the crowded, strenuous conditions of city life are indeed vital questions!
>
> To establish a home is one of the first objects of life! A home that shall be to us and our children the fountain source of inspiration and help in all the affairs of life! A place where our highest aspirations shall be stimulated, our best affection nurtured, and in which our memory will cling most fondly in all the years to come.
>
> The ideal home should be amid the trees with sunlight and air on all sides; fragrant with the scent of grass and leaves and growing flowers. All these things add to the charm of a home and are vital necessities to the full development of a natural, healthful child.
>
> Flatbush from the time of its first settlement by the Dutch in 1656 has been a section of ideal homes! The old Dutch home established here were homes of comfort, refinement and happiness! The virtues that were developed in those early homes produced the noble men and women known as the old residents of the Flatbush section. The Colonial homesteads, unpretentious yet roomy and comfortable, with their wide halls and spacious old-fashioned fireplaces, around which the family gathered in winter are passing away and giving place to the more modern homes of the twentieth century. The farms have been cut up into plots and all classes can find here a home suited to their means.

At 5:00 in the afternoon of July 2, 1878, the Brooklyn-Flatbush and Coney Island Railroad made its first run from its terminal at the Willink entrance of Prospect Park. Pulled by a steam engine named the *John A. Lott*, and with Judge John A. Lott of Flatbush on board, the first president of the company, the train arrived at the Brighton Beach Hotel on the Atlantic shore just fourteen minutes later. To celebrate the inaugural run Judge Lott hosted a large gala dinner. The celebration marked the beginning of what would evolve into the Brighton Beach Line of the BMT (the Brighton-Manhattan Transit Co.), one of the three major subway systems of New York City. Today, the Prospect Park station is an express stop on the Brighton Line and the terminus for the Franklin Avenue shuttle. The station's entrance on Flatbush

Avenue, just south of its junction with Ocean Avenue and Empire Boulevard (formerly Malbone Street), is not far from the Willink gate of Prospect Park and the original Brooklyn-Flatbush and Coney Island Railroad terminal.

Brooklyn-Flatbush and Coney Island Railroad began as an excursion, not a commuter, steam railroad that transported holiday-seeking passengers to the shore resorts of Brighton Beach and Coney Island. The company started with five steam engines and about forty wooden passenger cars. Most of the cars were enclosed, because the railroad operated year-round. However, some of the cars reserved for the warm weather were open and without sidewalls. Passengers sat on wooden benches and enjoyed the breezes as they traveled to the beaches and racetracks of southern Brooklyn.

Initially to reach the new rail line, which began at the Willink entrance to Prospect Park just outside the southern border of the city of Brooklyn, passengers coming from the city had to travel south on Flatbush Avenue from the Atlantic Terminal of the Long Island Railroad (still located in downtown Brooklyn at the junction of Atlantic and Flatbush Avenues) in the Brooklyn-Flatbush and Coney Island Company's horse-drawn street railroad cars. This arrangement made travel inconvenient. However, starting their routes at the margins of the city was, for several reasons, typical of the excursion steam railroads. First, gaining the right-of-ways in the more densely populated areas was costly; second, there was opposition from the many competing horse-drawn street railroad lines; and lastly, civic leaders and adjacent property owners opposed a steam engine running on grade on city streets as both a danger to pedestrians and because of the soot and pollution that it spewed. There was less of a hazard on the more sparsely populated route south of Brooklyn.

Although the steam engine was an important step in the development of the intra-urban transit system, the excursion railroads of Brooklyn would have to overcome serious obstacles in order to turn themselves into commuter lines. These required replacing steam engines with electric cars, eliminating dangerous grade crossings, and extending their routes into Manhattan. The story of how these problems were resolved by the Brooklyn-Flatbush and Coney Island Railroad as it evolved into the Brighton Line of today is a case in point.

Even as the Brooklyn-Flatbush and Coney Island Railroad was celebrating its inaugural run on July 2, 1878, the company was already engaged in building a connection to Brooklyn. It was completed in August 1878, under a contract negotiated with the Long Island Railroad. The extended route, much like the one followed by the Franklin Avenue shuttle today, required that the trains go east away from the park before turning north to climb up and over Crown Heights. From there the trains would pass through a tunnel dug under Eastern Parkway and travel to the Bedford Terminal, located at Franklin and Atlantic Avenues (where today's Franklin Avenue shuttle terminates.) At the Bedford Terminal the trains would enter the Long Island Railroad tracks for the short distance to the Atlantic Terminal at Flatbush and Atlantic Avenues in the heart of downtown Brooklyn. That link gave the new line an in-city terminal and a strong—although it turned out to be temporary—advantage over the other excursion railroads.

The Brooklyn-Flatbush and Coney Island Railroad underwent several bankruptcies and name, ownership, and route changes before Mayor Fiorello LaGuardia merged it into the New York City Transit System in 1940. (Today the NewYork State Metropolitan Transportation Authority, the MTA, operates the city's subway systems.) In 1896, then known as the Brooklyn and Brighton Beach Railroad, it affiliated with the Kings County Elevated Company and through use of their elevated tracks was able to extend its route to Sands Street at the foot of the Brooklyn Bridge. From there passengers could transfer to trains that crossed the bridge into Manhattan. With its new easy access to Manhattan, the railroad began operating as a commuter rather than excursion line.

In 1899 Brooklyn Rapid Transit (BRT), a politically well-connected private holding company, consolidated Brooklyn's many railroad and streetcar lines under its control. The company almost immediately ended the era of steam engines by electrifying all of its trains. The first electrification, which used overhead cables and trolleys, proved unsatisfactory. Later that system was replaced with the electrified third rail, the system still in use on all New York City subway lines. Although "trolley" became the generic name for the electrified streetcars that plied the streets of Brooklyn and other cities, the word trolley actually means the apparatus that connects the vehicle to overhead electric cables. Until grade crossings were eliminated from the Brighton line, however, it was too dangerous to use the more efficient electrified third rail—the present method for operating the subways—to run the trains.

At first BRT wanted to improve the Brighton line by having it run from Church Avenue to Sheepshead Bay on elevated tracks, the most cost-effective method. However, by 1905 middle-class developments bordering on the right of way—Caton Park, Prospect Park South, Beverly Square East and West, Ditmas Park, Ditmas Park West, Fisk Terrace, Midwood Park, and West Midwood—were already taking shape and the new homeowners vehemently and successfully protested the plan. Instead, an open trench sixteen feet deep and fifty feet wide and sufficiently wide enough to contain four tracks was dug from the Prospect Park Station to Avenue H. The trench, which was supported along its entire route from the Prospect Park station by reinforced concrete walls, contains six stations: Parkside Avenue, a local stop; Church Avenue, an express stop; Beverly and Cortelyou Roads, two local stops; Newkirk Avenue, an express stop; and Avenue H, a local stop. From Avenue H, the last stop in Flatbush, the train travels on elevated tracks to Brighton Beach and Coney Island. The importance of easy access to rapid transit was not lost on T.B. Ackerson, the builder of Beverly Square East and West, who, during the construction process, used his political clout to get both the Beverly Road and Cortelyou Road stations built. Those two local stops are one block apart, the closest subway stops in the system.

The approximate cost of the construction was $2,500,000, shared by the city that paid $1,000,000 and the railroad that paid $1,500,000. The reconstruction was done under the joint management of the Grade Crossing Commission, the official body in charge of eliminating grade crossings; the Brooklyn Rapid Transit lines, the railroad operator; and John H. Dwyer, the engineer. Charles Cranford was the contractor on the section that traversed Flatbush. Working in very tight space, his company was able to complete its work in eighteen months with minimum disruption to the heavily used railroad line and to neighborhoods along the route. At the end of the work, the people of Flatbush honored Cranford with a celebratory dinner.

During the summer and fall of 1918 labor troubles roiled the BRT. On November 1, 1918 the dispute culminated in a strike called by the Brotherhood of Locomotive Engineers, a union representing motormen and switchmen. About half the workforce joined the strike, throwing the morning rush hour into severe disarray. By the afternoon rush hour the company brought in replacement workers—other railroad employees neither experienced motormen nor switchmen—who, in anticipation of the possible strike, had hurriedly been given some very basic training in operating the trains.

At 6:42 pm that November evening, an inexperienced, overtired employee, unable to slow his five-car train speeding down a grade, lost control of it on a curve going into the Prospect Park station. The wooden train derailed. Ninety-three people were killed and many others were injured. Known as the Malbone Street wreck, the disaster remains one of the worst mass transit accidents in the city's history. The shock of the crash was so great that the city renamed Malbone Street to Empire Boulevard to help erase the memory of that dreadful night. The catastrophe broke the already financially troubled BRT's back, forcing the company into bankruptcy. When the company emerged from the bankruptcy in 1923 it had a new name, the BMT or Brooklyn-Manhattan Transit, signifying that the line had direct access into Manhattan. In Brooklyn, the current south to north route of the Brighton line, now designated as the Q (local) and B (express) trains, runs on elevated tracks from Coney Island to Avenue H, through Flatbush from Avenue H to Prospect Park in an open below-grade cut, from Prospect Park through a tunnel under Flatbush Avenue, then over the Manhattan Bridge into Manhattan. The Manhattan connection was completed in 1920.

Because of its location at the center of Brooklyn, Flatbush became an important hub of public street-level transportation. After the 1890s introduction of trolleys, at least five trolley lines criss-crossed Flatbush and transfers were possible from many other lines. For sixty-six years, until the last trolley was taken out of service in 1956, they were a ubiquitous presence. Even Brooklyn's beloved baseball team, the Brooklyn Dodgers, was originally known as the Trolley Dodgers, thus memorializing both the importance of the trolley car and their very real danger to pedestrians who constantly had to dodge them.

In 1864 Flatbush initiated another final infrastructure improvement critical to its transformation. In that year John A. Lott, John Lefferts, John J. Vanderbilt, Henry Wall, Homer L. Bartlett, and Abraham Lott formed the Flatbush Gas Company. The gas plant was located on Clarkson Avenue near the old Clove Road. And in 1893 the new Knickerbocker Electric Light and Power Company, which was quickly bought by the Flatbush Gas Company, was given a fifteen-year contract by the town board to supply electric arc street lamps for the town. Under the supervision of C.C. Martin, an engineer, an electric plant was built in 1894. In 1897 the Brooklyn Union

Gas Company, which today continues to operate as Keyspan Energy Corporation, purchased the stock of the Flatbush Gas Company. The new company greatly improved service by laying many more gas and electric lines. Beginning in the early twentieth century, gas and electric services were provided to individual homes.

The Churches

Another sign of Flatbush's growth and change was the formation and construction of new churches. For almost 200 years the Reformed Dutch Church of Flatbush had met the spiritual needs of the community and accommodated people of other Protestant denominations. But by early in the nineteenth century, as more and more people made their homes in Flatbush, the population of the town grew more religiously diverse. The church of one Protestant denomination was no longer sufficient to meet the spiritual or social needs of the community. Beginning in 1836 new congregations were formed and new churches built. By 1880 there were seven churches in Flatbush, and by 1920 the number had grown to more than twenty-five and included Jewish congregations. In addition to meeting the spiritual needs of their congregants, these churches and synagogues through their various organizations, including men's clubs, women's clubs, youth clubs, and service societies, contributed to the social infrastructure of the rapidly developing Flatbush communities. The growth in church membership reflected the desirability of Flatbush as a residential community and helped to accelerate its evolution from an ingrown farming enclave into a diverse urban suburb. The vitality and energy of the "new" Flatbush also attracted a college-educated, seminary-trained clergy. Although it is not possible to consider here all the new congregations established between the mid-nineteenth century and the early years of the twentieth century, it is important to understand Flatbush's rising diversity of religious communities; a harbinger of the later explosion of the multiple ethnicities that washed through the neighborhood.

The first new congregation was St. Paul's Episcopal Church of Flatbush. Organized in 1836, it represented the increasing presence of Anglo-Americans in Flatbush. In keeping with its liberal traditions the Flatbush Reformed Dutch Church allowed its consistory room to be used by the new church until its own building was completed. The cornerstone for St. Paul's was laid in August 1836 with the Right Reverend B.T. Onderdonk, Bishop of the Diocese of New York, and Reverend Benjamin C. Cutler, D.D. presiding. A month earlier the first vestry, consisting of wardens Matthew Clarkson and Robert J. Crommelin, and vestrymen David Johnson, James Mowatt, George Cornell, C. Durand, Charles Waldron, A. Norrie, William H. Story, and Samuel Richards Jr., was established. According to Reverend Strong, the building, including its organ, cost $8,480; $2,398 was raised by subscription. Matthew Clarkson, Esquire, one of the most prominent English residents of Flatbush, contributed both the land and the remaining $6,082. On December 23, 1836 Reverend Thomas S. Brittain was chosen the first rector. The church was consecrated the following week, on December 29. Its present stone building, designed by architect Herbert Brewster, stands at the corner of St. Paul's Court and St. Paul's Place. It was dedicated in 1902.

Shortly after the first St. Paul's building opened its doors in 1838, a small Methodist Church (it later became Congregational) appears on the 1842 map (see chapter three), located at the eastern end of town between Flatbush and New Lots. The church, according to Reverend Strong, served the African-American population of the two towns. Its first elder was the Reverend Samuel Todd.

In 1849 a Methodist-Episcopal Church was built at Church Avenue and Prospect Street, east of Flatbush Avenue. Its less affluent congregation gathered in the warm months of 1844 under unusual circumstances. In that year ministers and itinerant preachers of the faith began preaching under the old Linden tree that stood on Church Avenue near Flatbush Avenue, in front of what was once the old Zabriskie house (see chapter three) and was later the site of the RKO Kenmore Theater. In the winter the service was moved indoors and held in the home of Rem Hegeman. Hegeman, a mechanic and builder, supervised the construction of the new church building.

Not far away, near the more affluent community of Beverly Square East, St. Mark's, the second Methodist-Episcopal church in the area, held its first services in the Jahn Mansion at Beverly Road and Ocean Avenue in 1903. By 1904 the congregation was able to break ground for a permanent building on the same site. The handsome building, completed in 1906 at a cost of $125,000, has a gray granite façade trimmed with Indiana limestone. During construction the congregation experienced rapid growth and by the time the new building opened it had 600 members and a Sunday school of 500. Lewis H. Pounds (1861–1947), one of the developers of Beverly Square East, and later the developer of Ditmas Park, was one of the founding trustees.

The first Roman Catholic Church services in Flatbush, led by Fathers John Quinn and Edward Briody, for a growing Irish-American population on the east side of Flatbush Avenue, were held in 1848 at the old Curran house that stood inside the Holy Cross Cemetery. In 1852 the Holy Cross Roman Catholic Church, initially a wood frame structure located at Erasmus and Prospect Streets, was built. Father Bacon, who later became the Bishop of Portland, Maine, conducted the first mass at the new building. By 1883 when Father R.J. Woods arrived the original wood structure had been replaced by one of stone. In addition to reducing the large mortgage, Father Woods added the first parochial school in 1900, built a new rectory for the priests, and constructed a convent for the sisters. In 1909 Holy Innocents, the second R.C. Church in Flatbush, opened its doors at Beverly Road and East 17th Street. A few years later, in 1914, it too added a parochial school. A third church, Our Lady of Refuge R.C., located at Foster and Ocean Avenues and not far from Holy Innocents, was built in 1911. It also has a parochial school next door. Today, Our Lady of Refuge conducts mass in three languages: English; French-Creole, for its Haitian parishioners; and Spanish for its Latino parishioners.

In 1871 the Reformed Dutch Grace Chapel at Flatbush Avenue and Grand Street was built. It evolved from a Sunday school that was started in 1856 for children who were descendents of slaves. The original Sunday school was supported by the Society for the Amelioration of the Colored Population of Flatbush, a charitable organization that was associated with the First Dutch Reformed Church. At the turn of the century when the consistory of the church decided to organize the chapel into a church, it called as its pastor the Reverend Charles S. Wyckoff who, as a direct descendant of prominent early settler Peter Claesen Wyckoff, had deep roots in the community.

In the same year, the First Baptist Church of Flatbush began holding meetings at Schoonmaker's Hall at 893 Flatbush Avenue. The Dutch Reformed Church leased the congregation land at 544 Ocean Avenue for the first church they called "The Tabernacle." In 1888 the church moved to a permanent building at Lenox Road and Nostrand Avenue at the eastern end of Flatbush. At the time some members felt they were moving "into the woods." At the turn of the century another Baptist Church, The Church of the Redeemer, was built at Cortelyou Road and East 18th Street. This congregation evolved from prayer meetings held in members' homes. When its building was completed in 1901, the church had forty-two members. Seven years later, in 1908, it had grown to 350 members.

The Flatbush-Tompkins Congregational Church, located in Ditmas Park at East 18th Street and Dorchester Road, was established in 1899. The well-to-do people largely responsible for founding it were Mr. and Mrs. Edward Basset who, before they moved to Flatbush, had been members of the Tompkins Avenue Congregational Church in what is now Bedford Stuyvesant, and Mr. and Mrs. Franklin Selleck, who had moved to Flatbush from Buffalo. The church began with thirty-nine members; Katherine, Mary, and Helen McCreary of Flatbush, former members of the Tompkins Church, were the first to join. Reverend C. Thurston Chase was the first pastor, serving until 1906. Until the congregation could move to its new building, an unusual eight-sided, shingled structure designed by the architectural firm of Whitefield and King, services were held at the Masonic Lodge on Flatbush Avenue between Caton and Church Avenues. In 1910 the well-known Boston architectural firm of Francis R. Allen (1843–1931) and Charles Collens (d. 1956), the architects of the Union Theological Seminary in Manhattan, in collaboration with local architect Louis Jallade, designed the current building that the New York City Landmark's Commission considers "one of the City's finest new-Georgian Churches." The church is active in community affairs and is the starting point of the annual Victorian Flatbush House Tour. The original building, on East 18th Street near Ditmas Avenue and now the Iglisia Bautista of Flatbush, serves a mostly Latino population.

In 1905 All Souls Universalist Church moved to Flatbush from South Second Street in Williamsburg Brooklyn, where it had been founded in 1845. In Flatbush it joined with the Church of Divine Love that it had organized several years earlier. The well-known architect John J. Petit (1870–1923) who had been the principal architect for Prospect Park South and in other parts of Flatbush as well, designed the Italian Mission style building on the corner of Ocean and Ditmas Avenues. The church had more than twenty stained glass windows, two designed by Tiffany, the others designed by J.&R. Lamb. In the early part of the twentieth century this church grew rapidly and played an active role in community affairs. Among its lasting contributions was the publication of three books, *The Realm of Light and Air*, *The Midwouter*, and *Flatbush of Today*, all of which provide valuable insights into everyday life in early twentieth-century Flatbush. The volume *Flatbush Today* was published in conjunction with a festival, held the week of April 27 to May 2, 1908 to celebrate the tricentennial of the Dutch arrival in Flatbush. Today the building, with its large grounds, is the Eglise Wesleyenne des Pilgrims, serving Flatbush's growing Haitian community.

One of the first Boy Scout troops in Brooklyn was organized at the small chapel that was the first home of the Wells Memorial Presbyterian Church. The church, founded in 1906, began in a storefront on Argyle Road, near Coney Island Avenue, and was the first church in what is now West Midwood, but was then a sparsely populated area at the west end of Flatbush. It later moved to a wooden structure at Glenwood and Argyle Roads, and finally to its stone building opposite the earlier building. Recently the church building was sold to the Church of Jesus Christ of Latter-Day Saints, a Mormon group new to the area.

In the early twentieth century there was a large Jewish migration to Flatbush from the Lower East Side, and the Williamsburg, East New York, and Brownsville sections of Brooklyn. Like other groups before them, they too felt the need for their own houses of worship. In 1908 Hannah Hirsch, a mother who wanted to supplement her children's public school education with religious training, brought together thirty-five Jewish families who founded Temple Beth Emeth (House of Truth), a Reformed temple. The Reformed movement is the least restrictive branch of Judaism. The other two branches of Judaism, Conservative, and the most traditional—Orthodox, also established synagogues in the area.

At first, the Hirsch group ran a small Jewish school that met every Sunday at Dillard's French Bakery Shop and Dining Room on Cortelyou Road. Finally, in 1911, they decided to build the Beth Emeth synagogue. The new temple opened in 1914 and marked the beginning of organized Jewish activities in Flatbush.

The founding families acquired land at Marlborough Road and Church Avenue, but met strong opposition from the surrounding property owners in Prospect Park South. The problem was resolved amicably when it was agreed to set the building back from Marlborough Road and the architectural firm of Eisendrath and Horowitz, known for their synagogue designs, designed a structure acceptable to the community. Until the new building was completed in 1914, services were held a few blocks away at the Unitarian Church at Beverly Road and East 19th Street. By 1921 the congregation had outgrown its space and in order to expand purchased adjoining property on Marlborough Road. Again property owners objected, but this time the matter was litigated. The court settled the matter in favor of the temple.

By mid-century Beth Emeth had a membership of over 2,000 families and other synagogues, Reformed, Conservative, and Orthodox also thrived. By the end of the century, although a growing Orthodox Jewish community flourished in the neighboring areas of Midwood and Borough Park, the Reformed synagogues of Flatbush lost membership as congregants moved away. Today Beth Emeth is the only remaining Reformed temple in Flatbush, and includes the remnants of three other congregations: Temple V'Ohr, the Progressive Synagogue, and Shaari Zadek.

In 1972 the Albanian American Islamic Center purchased an old mansion at

Rugby and Albemarle Roads in Prospect Park South and converted it into a mosque. Although the community does not live in the immediate area, the mosque operates on behalf of Albanian Americans and is an active center of their communal life. It also serves as a house of worship for a diverse population of area Moslems.

The Victorian Flatbush Neighborhoods

Today Flatbush is a distinctive area at the center of Brooklyn and encompasses a collection of different neighborhoods, each with its own history. The evolution of Flatbush from a farming community into a town began in 1834 when several English tradesmen and mechanics bought small lots in the area of what is now Erasmus and Johnson Streets on the east side of Flatbush Avenue. As more non-farmer tradesmen moved in, the area became known as the English Neighborhood. Recognizing the potential for profit, Dutch-descended Adrian Vanderveer in 1835 divided his farm near the English Neighborhood into building lots. Although neither the English Neighborhood nor the Vanderveer lots were recorded on Reverend Strong's 1842 map (see chapter three), Vanderveer was criticized by some of his neighbors for subdividing his land. By the 1860s the new, faster transit lines that were reaching Flatbush helped to create a market for new housing. At that time a large number of small frame houses were built on the Vanderveer lots. An 1873 real estate map shows a pattern of developed streets and a growing population on the east side of Flatbush Avenue. The area on the west side remained mostly as farmland and was only developed into residential neighborhoods later.

By the beginning of the twentieth century it was clear Flatbush Avenue had become a dividing line, with most of the wealthier areas, now collectively known as Victorian Flatbush, to its west and the more working class neighborhoods on its east. Writing in the publication *Realm of Light and Air*, the Honorable John Z. Lott, son of Judge John A. Lott and a community leader of the "new" western Flatbush, commented on the growing popularity of the area as a residential choice of the well-to-do and called attention to the uneven development that he viewed as positive.

> Judging from the tendencies of present development, the east side of town will be largely devoted to the erection of brick and stone flats and private dwellings. There would seem, however, to be enough restricted property on the west side, between Flatbush and Coney Island Avenues, to hold the fine character of development already started. It would seem, therefore, that the result in the future there will be a choice of high-grade detached residential sections without undue congestion, surrounded by a modern city. This done should make the values in both sections referred to very high and the section very popular.

The developers who bought the farmland on the west side of Flatbush Avenue for residential development did more than simply build houses. They had a vision. They wanted to build safe and social communities for a refined and cultured Protestant middle class—essentially the early twentieth-century complement to the patrician population that they were replacing. This attitude was summed up by Dean Alvord, the developer of Prospect Park South, one of the earliest, perhaps grandest of the neighborhoods, and with its design innovations a model for the communities that would follow. Accordingly its sales prospectus, written by Alvord, emphasized the safety and homogeneity of the area: "In fixing upon a location for a home, it is pleasant to live where children, in going to and fro are not subject to the annoyance of contact with undesirable elements of society. The Flatbush Avenue trolley line penetrates no slum sections and is patronized almost exclusively by people of intelligence and good breeding."

Lewis H. Pounds, the developer of Ditmas Park and Ditmas Park West, echoed Alvord's sentiments. In his view the developer and the residents of the neighborhoods had a moral responsibility to each other and to their community. It was the responsibility of the developer, Pounds wrote in *Flatbush of Today*, "to select the original residents and mold the character of the neighborhood." The responsibility of the residents, according to Pounds, was to maintain and beautify their property.

> The people who have made Ditmas Park and Ditmas Park West their homes have to a large extent realized their own part in this dual responsibility. They have cooperated in the maintaining and beautifying their residences and grounds. They have had the neighborly spirit, which is more than a social trait, and more than the expression of personal pride. It has extended to the protection of the neighbor and the neighborhood in refusals to sell their residences to people of a lower grade, and who would have nothing in common with those about them. . . . There are many instances where builder and homeowner have refused most attractive prices simply because the character of the purchaser was not up to the standard of the neighborhood.

In order to carry out their image of a proper neighborhood the developers first had to level open fields and change them into an urban streetscape. An 1869 New York state law imposed a street grid, a rigid plan of straight vertical and horizontal streets that crossed each other at right angles. Flatbush Avenue, which skewed east, was the exception. However, the rigidity of the grid restricted the developers' design options. Before building could begin, they had to lay out the building lots and add sewer and underground utility lines. Some developers designed their own houses, others worked with an architect, still others sold the lots to other builders, and some allowed lot owners to hire their own architects. Nevertheless, in order to maintain some sense of cohesiveness they all set conditions for the development that always included setbacks from the street and often uniform roof heights as well.

The developers also had to sell the idea of private homeownership in suburban Flatbush as opposed to apartment living—being a cliff dweller as one writer put it—in Manhattan. One of the strongest boosters of Flatbush was the First Universalist Church, whose publications not only extolled its virtues, but also helped to instruct young people on how to finance a home. The church too was interested in attracting "proper" middle-class families to the new, elite neighborhoods. Writing in the Universalist Church publication *The Realm of Light and Air*, Flatbush born W.A.A. Brown, one of Flatbush's leading real estate developers and brokers, encouraged young families to purchase a home. "The cost of buying a house has been made by the builders about as easy as paying rent," he wrote, adding that, "if the young man has an income large enough to rent a first-class apartment in the city, he has enough capital to start a bona-fide home of his own in Flatbush." John L. Heaton, a businessman, writing in the same publication, calculated the expenses:

> Take for example a young man who has $5,000 saved and drawing interest at 4 per cent., and who is now paying $1,000 rent [per year] in Manhattan. He buys a $10,000 house, assuming a $5,000 mortgage, with interest at $5^{1/2}$ per cent., including tax. His carrying cost is therefore $4^{3/4}$ per cent., average, for interest, plus three per cent. for all the other charges combined, or $7^{3/4}$ per cent.—in all $775 per year. In the example given the young man saves $225 a year, which he should either invest or apply to extinguishing the mortgage. He is that much ahead.

"Testing their own finances by this rule," Heaton concluded, "almost any thrifty young couple will find that they can easily afford a house instead of a flat in a cliff-side. The real question is whether they wish it."

An added inducement to living in Flatbush was its neighborliness and sociability, as well as the comforts of a spacious home and garden. In turn-of-the-century Flatbush, social life was centered in the home, the neighborhoods, and around three clubs. All of the most prominent families claimed membership in at least one. The oldest of the "country" clubs was the Midwood Club, founded in 1889. Many of its founders were members of the old Flatbush families, including John Z. Lott, John Lefferts Vandebilt, Dr. Homer L. Bartlett, and William K. Clarkson. Others like William A.A. Brown, Richard Ficken, Edward F. Selding, Henry Sherrill, and Gustav Jahn represented the "new" elite. The club purchased the old Matthew Clarkson residence that had been built in 1836 and was one of the remaining examples of the old English-American architecture that had once dominated Flatbush. Although the building was "modernized" to meet the needs of club members, much of the exterior and interior décor was kept intact. According to a 1908 description, the building's "great hall, beautiful winding staircase, magnificent drawing-rooms, ladies' parlor and well-equipped library with their open fireplaces and finely carved marble mantels speak of other days, but the upper rooms have been made over into modern billiard, pool and card rooms and a café."

The basement of the club housed bowling alleys and the "log cabin" room, a fraternal meeting place for men.

The Knickerbocker Field Club was also founded in 1889 as a lawn tennis club. It is located at East 18th Street and Albemarle Road (then known as Avenue A) on land leased from Richard Friken, the builder of Tennis Court, one of the earliest developments of large freestanding homes. The club grew quickly and a large, well-equipped clubhouse, including bowling alleys and an auditorium seating 400 to accommodate a drama group, was built. The clubhouse burned down in the 1980s. However, the Knickerbocker Club still has an active membership of Brooklyn tennis players.

The last of the Flatbush social clubs, the Cortelyou Club, was organized in 1896. It was located on the site of the old Cortelyou homestead at the junction of Bedford, Newkirk, and Ditmas Avenues, then a rapidly growing area. If the Midwood Club accommodated the more patrician members of Flatbush society, and the Knickerbocker Club emphasized athletics and theater, the Cortelyou Club made patriotism and social duty an important part of its agenda. It strongly supported members who enlisted in the Spanish American War by exempting them from dues and continuing them in good standing. Like the Knickerbocker Club, it too supported a members' theater group and provided other public entertainments.

In addition to the social clubs, Flatbush had an active 29th ward Republican Club, lead by Lewis H. Pounds, the developer of Ditmas Park and Ditmas Park West, and the Roosevelt Club composed of young Republicans. Pounds, who played an active role in Brooklyn politics, was elected Brooklyn Borough President (1913–1917) and New York State treasurer in 1924. He ran unsuccessfully for New York City mayor in 1932. The Republican homeowners also organized the Flatbush Taxpayers Association in 1896. By 1908 it had become the largest single taxpayers' or civic association in greater New York. The Democrats, who at that time were in the minority, had their headquarters at Flatbush Avenue and Lenox Road. By the 1930s, however, the arrival of large numbers of new working people, many of recent immigrant origin, changed the politics of Flatbush. The Democratic Party became dominant and, even today, almost totally eclipses the Republican presence.

Nevertheless, in spite of all their efforts, the communities as the developers envisioned them were short-lived. For many of the original "new" families, Flatbush proved to be a way station and they soon moved on to more distant suburbs. By the 1920s the first wave of upwardly mobile immigrants and first-generation Americans were moving into Flatbush. Most moved into the large six-story elevator high rises and four-story walk-up multifamily houses that were beginning to line Ocean Avenue. These new people of various ethnic and religious backgrounds brought to Flatbush the vital energy and vibrancy that turned it into a quintessential urban place and were the source of legendary Flatbush.

Ocean Avenue, to the west of Flatbush Avenue, is one of the major thoroughfares. It begins at the junction of Empire Boulevard and Flatbush Avenue, near the Willink entrance to Prospect Park and runs along the east side of the park to Parkside Avenue. From there it continues parallel to Coney Island Avenue, ten blocks to its west. Unlike Coney Island and Flatbush Avenues, which are busy commercial streets, Ocean Avenue is almost entirely residential. Early in the twentieth century it was lined with large one-family houses and churches. By 1920 almost all of the single-family houses were gone and it had become a street of mostly six-story art deco apartment buildings.

One of the most distinctive buildings is located on the northwest corner of Beverly Road. Built for the Vitograph studio during the heyday of motion picture production in Brooklyn, it was the home to many of the Vitograph stars, including Mary Pickford, Fatty Arbuckle, and Douglas Fairbanks Sr., who lived in the penthouse. The studio later built a private house on the southwest corner of Rugby Road and Ditmas Avenue in Ditmas Park West, for Mary Pickford. However, almost as soon as it was completed the motion picture industry left Brooklyn for Hollywood.

Most of the planned single-family home communities are west of Flatbush Avenue, but the exception is Prospect Lefferts Gardens. This community is located on the east side of Flatbush Avenue, at the northern tip of Flatbush, and is not considered one of the Victorian Flatbush neighborhoods. Anticipating that high-grade residential developments would soon be built, James Lefferts in 1893 supervised the division of the Lefferts family land holdings into 600 lots he called Lefferts Manor. From east to west Lefferts Manor is two blocks wide and north to south it is five blocks deep. The east side of Flatbush Avenue is its western boundary and Rogers Avenue is its eastern border; Lincoln Road is the northern boundary; followed by Maple Street, Midwood Street, Rutland Road, and Fenimore Street as its southern border. Today, the original Lefferts Manor is the Lefferts part of the name of a larger, though architecturally harmonious area known as Prospect-Lefferts Gardens. The Prospect and Gardens part of the name comes from its proximity to Prospect Park (near the Willink gate) and the nearby Brooklyn Botanic Gardens. In 1979 the New York City Landmarks Preservation Commission designated Prospect-Lefferts Gardens as a Historic District.

Under the terms of the original sale, Lefferts, who hoped to attract a stable middle-class population, tried to protect the residential character of the area by barring farming, manufacturing, and industrial uses. He prohibited "stables, pigpens, forges, iron foundries, [the manufacture of] fertilizer, gunpowder, soap, candles, ink, glue and varnish factories, tanneries, breweries etc." He also banned hospitals, theaters, apartment houses, tenements "or any noxious, offensive, dangerous, unwholesome business whatsoever." In addition, Lefferts attached restrictive covenants to each lot requiring that each house cost no less than $5,000 to build, be single-family, be built of brick or stone (a provision not fully adhered to), stand at least two stories high and have a cellar, be set back fourteen feet from the street, and that all stables and outbuildings be at least sixty feet from the street. Unlike the suburban, park-like aesthetic of most of the planned neighborhoods to its south, the architecture of Lefferts Manor and the larger area of Prospect-Lefferts Gardens is decidedly urban, smaller versions of the row "brownstone" houses found in the residential neighborhoods north of Prospect Park.

In spite of Lefferts's efforts during the mid-1890s, sales were slow and the area remained sparsely built. The first significant development took place between 1897 and 1899 when the real estate developer William A.A. Brown put up 160 buildings. Some of these houses, which were advertised in 1898, were not purchased until six or seven years later. An additional 507 houses, most built by the firm of Frederick

Norris & Company, were constructed in the larger area between 1905 and 1911; eighty-seven more houses were added between 1915 and 1925. Later, some larger, freestanding one-family houses were built along Maple Street between 1922 and 1927. Outside of Lefferts Manor, where Lefferts's restrictions did not apply, some of the houses, although they fit into the streetscape because they used a single entrance, were built for two families.

Like many of the neighborhoods in Flatbush, Prospect-Lefferts Gardens was able to survive the ravages of time, although not unscathed. It has seen some of its original housing torn down and replaced by large apartment houses; it has also weathered the Depression and the post–World War II rush to the suburbs of Long Island, Westchester, and New Jersey. Nevertheless, the neighborhood held on, in no small measure because of the work of the Lefferts Manor Neighborhood Association, formed in 1919. The association, which has melded into a larger Prospect-Lefferts Gardens Association, actively worked to maintain the character of the neighborhood and preserve the original residential restrictions of James Lefferts. Today Prospect-Lefferts Gardens, which was helped by the influx of new young families during the 1960s and 1970s, is a close-knit, active, well-integrated community of white, black, Caribbean, and Asian homeowners. The landmark status assures that its architectural integrity and ambiance will be preserved.

South of Prospect-Lefferts Gardens, on the east side of Ocean Avenue, is Albemarle-Kenmore Terrace, an enclave of single-family low-rise homes amid the six-story multi-family apartment houses that dominate the surrounding area between Ocean and Flatbush Avenues. The Albemarle-Kenmore Terrace area consists of two small mews blocks, located off East 21st Street between Church Avenue and Albemarle Road. Although considered part of Victorian Flatbush, the architectural styles of these two small developments of attached row houses are more urban than suburban.

In 1916 Mabel Bull purchased the land on which Albemarle-Kenmore Terrace sits. The land had originally been part of the Bergen farm, although at the time of the purchase the Lott family owned it. Bull hired the real estate firm of Midwood Associates to develop Albemarle Terrace. They in turn hired the architectural firm of John Bay Slee (1875–1947) and Robert H. Bryson (1875–1938), who were among the more prolific architects in Flatbush. They built Albemarle Terrace, which consists of attached brick and limestone neo-Federal houses, raised above street level and set behind a terrace. Construction began in 1916 was completed in 1917.

Development of the south side of the adjacent Kenmore Terrace, also owned by Mabel Bull, was begun a year later in 1918 and completed in 1919. These houses show the strong influence of the English Garden City movement, an architectural approach that sought to combine the best of urban and suburban development with modern sensibilities. In the United States the movement was contemporaneous with the rise of the automobile culture, and this was acknowledged in Kenmore Terrace, one of the first developments in New York City to attach garages to homes. The north side of Kenmore Terrace is still owned by the First Reformed Dutch Church. The church's Parish House and Parsonage, built in 1853 and moved from its original site on Flatbush

Avenue, are located there. Albemarle-Kenmore Terrace was designated as a Historic District in 1978 by the New York City Landmarks Preservation Commission.

The prototype for the remaining ten neighborhoods of Victorian Flatbush—communities built within very specific boundaries where the construction and sale of the houses could be carefully controlled—was Tennis Court, built in 1886 by Richard Friken. Friken made the necessary improvements to the land that included putting down water pipes, paving the streets and sidewalks, and planting trees. He then divided the land into fifty-foot wide lots for large, freestanding, suburban type houses. Like James Lefferts before him, he stipulated a minimum building cost for the houses of no less than $6,000. Friken sold his lots in 1887 for $1,500 each. The popularity of large freestanding houses pushed up the price of the lots, so that by 1899 they were selling for at least $5,000 exclusive of improvements. Fortune did not favor Tennis Court, which did not have a long life. In the 1920s many of the homes along Ocean Avenue, including those in Tennis Court, were torn down and replaced by elevated six-story multi-family apartment houses.

Each of the neighborhoods of Victorian Flatbush is distinctive. They were designed by different architects and built by different builders, all of whom imprinted them with a distinctive aesthetic. Nevertheless, they share much in common, including the anti-urban bias—a reaction against the blocks of row houses that characterized the residential areas of Brooklyn north of the park and Manhattan. Although originally built as commuter suburbs for the middle class, they continue to retain within their collective memory an echo of their pastoral Dutch roots.

These neighborhoods all have large freestanding homes with broad porches, set back from the street in private gardens surrounded by trees; they were all built at about the same time, between 1899 and 1920; each has an active neighborhood association that is almost as old as the neighborhood. The associations all work together on common concerns through the umbrella of the Flatbush Development Corporation. With the exception of one, South Midwood, they are located between Ocean Avenue on the east and Coney Island Avenue on the west. Although they have seen hard times, particularly at mid-century from the 1950s to the 1970s, a period of great upheaval and change in Brooklyn, these neighborhoods of large freestanding houses, with the exception of the incursion of some high-rise apartment buildings, have remained well preserved. Today, revitalized and renewed, they are vibrant, integrated communities that still maintain their older civic culture and neighborhood spirit.

Traveling from north to south, Victorian Flatbush begins with Caton Park, which is located just south of the Parade Grounds. Separated from Prospect Park by Parkside Avenue, they are public ballfields on what was once land belonging to the Martense family and is now a New York City park. The Parade Grounds are bordered on the north by Prospect Park, on the east by Parade Place, on the south by Caton Avenue, and on the west by Coney Island Avenue. They were built contemporaneously with the park and meant to protect its green lawns by providing open space for marching bands and drill teams. Almost from the beginning, however, they were used as playing fields. Among sports stars who began their careers playing there are Brooklyn-born baseball greats Sandy Koufax, Joe Torre, John Franco, and Lee Mazilli. In the spring of 2004 all eleven of these heavily used fields were reopened after a major renovation. They include two baseball diamonds built to major league specifications; two softball fields, a state of the art football field covered with artificial turf, and a soccer field. The other six fields, covered with artificial turf, are general purpose and can be used year round. Today, within a very tight schedule they accommodate the teams of organized amateur youth and adult baseball, football, soccer, and cricket leagues.

Caton Park, across Caton Avenue from the Parade Grounds, is one of the smallest and most endangered of the Victorian Flatbush neighborhoods. It is one block deep and three blocks wide, bordered by Caton Avenue on the north, Buckingham Road on the east, Church Avenue on the south, and Rugby Road on the west. It is also the least planned, built between 1902 and 1909 by three major Flatbush developers who worked independently of each other. The developers were John C. Sawkins, one of the most prolific builders of public and private structures throughout Flatbush, who built most of the houses; W.A.A. Brown, a prominent developer with offices nearby on Flatbush Avenue built along Marlborough Road; and Edward R. Strong, one of the youngest builder-developers, who worked on Rugby Road.

Today Caton Park has about fifty houses, having lost twelve in 1951 when Public School 249 was built on Caton Avenue between Rugby and Marlborough Roads. Other houses on Buckingham Road were lost to new low-rise and multi-family structures. The neighborhood fears losing additional houses as expansion-minded businesses along Church Avenue try to acquire houses for their land. The active Caton Park Association has been fighting to prevent the incursions and is considering applying for landmark status in order to preserve its architectural integrity.

In 1899 Dean Alvord (1856–1941), a real estate developer, purchased fifty acres of land from the First Reformed Church and the Bergen family for $280,000 and set out, he said, "to create a rural park within the limitations of the conventional city block and city street." His model was Prospect Park and he intended to extend the aesthetic of its creators, Frederick Law Olmsted and Calvin Vaux, to the city grid in his new development, which he named Prospect Park South.

Alvord, who came to Brooklyn from Rochester, New York where he gained experience building upscale suburban housing, meticulously planned the development of Prospect Park South as a totality. Writing in *Flatbush of Today*, and referring to himself in the third person, he explained:

> The one consideration which dominated the mind of the founder of Prospect Park South was that it should be treated as a whole and not as a collection of units. Every lot, street, park and building was studied in its relation to the whole property, just as an artist regards every stroke of his brush on a canvas. In this way there has been produced an ensemble without discord, and it is that feeling of harmony throughout which gives to Prospect Park South its unrivalled claim as Brooklyn's most beautiful residence park.

Prospect Park South is two blocks wide north to south and five blocks deep west to east. It is bordered on the north by Church Avenue and on the south by Beverly Road. The Brighton line subway is its eastern boundary; Coney Island Avenue forms it western border followed by Stratford, Westminster, Argyle, Rugby, Marlborough, and Buckingham Roads, originally numbered streets that Alvord replaced with what he considered to be typical upper-class English names. Thus, from west to east, East 12th Street became Stratford Road, East 13th Street became Argyle Road, East 14th Street became Rugby Road, East 15th Street became Marlborough Road, and East 16th Street became Buckingham Road. These new street names, with the exception of Buckingham Road, which because of the subway cut is only two blocks long, extend through several of the Victorian Flatbush neighborhoods before they revert back to being numbered streets.

At the center of Prospect Park South, running parallel to Church Avenue and Beverly Road, is Albemarle Road. Created as an elegant promenade, it is a wide street with a planted mall between its two roadways. Before it was removed a footbridge crossed above the tracks at Lewis Circle, at the end of Albemarle Road. A second planted mall is located on Buckingham Road. Like the earlier development of Tennis Court, Alvord used brick stanchions bearing medallions with the initials PPS to mark the entrance to every block in Prospect Park South at its borders along Church Avenue and Beverly Road.

Upon acquiring the land, Alvord worked with prolific architect John J. Petit, who designed many of the houses in a variety of architectural styles, and landscape gardener John Aitkin on every detail of the development. In order to maintain the park-like atmosphere Alvord required a uniform setback and roof level for the houses, building lots had to have a minimum frontage of fifty feet, and they had to cost no less than $5,000 to build. In order to maintain the openness of the area, fences were forbidden and hedges could only be planted for privacy in the backyards. Sidewalks were moved closer to the building line, and eight-foot-wide planted strips between the sidewalk and the street were placed in front of every house. To give the impression of an even wider expanse, trees were planted along the property line, not as they usually are along the curb. Two types of trees were planted, fast-growing but short-lived Carolina poplars were planted for immediate shade, and the slower-growing, but long-living Norway maples were planted for long-term shade. In the last few years these Norway maples have reached the end of their life span, and they are slowly dying and being cut down.

On designating Prospect Park South a Historic District, the New York City Landmarks Preservation Commission noted that the seemingly random mixing of various architectural styles was part of a new phenomenon becoming common in American suburbs at the turn of the twentieth century. It was a sharp break with the older architectural aesthetic that made style more site-specific and dependent on its surroundings. The design of Prospect Park South and most of its sister neighborhoods broke with this convention. According to the commission's report:

> The buildings erected in these developments represent an eclectic mix with houses of many different styles placed next to each other on each street. Each house at Prospect Park South was designed as a separate entity with no consideration given to the style of the surrounding structures or to the appropriateness of the use of a certain stylistic variant at a specific site. . . . At Prospect Park South houses with Colonial, Queen Anne, Italianate, French Renaissance, Japanese . . . and other stylistic details were freely juxtaposed. This free mixture of stylistic forms often resulted in such seeming incongruities as the placement of a stucco Spanish Mission style home beside a frame Swiss Chalet. A rustic Swiss Chalet style design would seem to be more appropriate to a rugged mountainous area and a Spanish Mission style building to the landscape of the southwest and not to the flat street grid of Flatbush. At Prospect Park South the styles of these houses have been removed from their original contexts and comfortably juxtaposed together. In the mid-nineteenth century such a juxtaposition of houses of varying styles would have been deemed to be totally inappropriate, but by 1900 this stylistic mix had gained acceptance and was seen as an enlivening factor.

Alvord, who checked the references of all potential buyers, succeeded in attracting wealthy, Protestant business and financial people who were seeking a comfortable life. He required homeowners pay a fee towards the upkeep of the common gardens and malls. In 1905 the Prospect Park South Association was established. Its primary mission was to conserve the neighborhood. Today most of the 208 property owners in Prospect Park South voluntarily pay dues to the Prospect Park South Association to maintain the malls on Albemarle and Buckingham Roads and the planted curb strips along every street. Recently, with a grant from the city obtained by Councilwoman Yvette Clarke, the association is working to restore the original streetscape by replacing the modern lampposts with replicas of the originals. In addition, the association holds a number of popular social events including an annual Know Your Neighbor Night; progressive dinners where neighbors meet for cocktails at one house, eat a full dinner at other houses, and regroup for dessert at a third house; a children's Halloween parade and party; holiday caroling; and wine tastings.

Prospect Park South was designated a Historic District by the New York City Landmarks Preservation Commission in 1979 and is listed on the National Register of Historic Places. It has also served as a model for the communities that developed to its south.

South of Prospect Park South are the contiguous neighborhoods of Beverly Square East and Beverly Square West that were developed by the architect and builder T.B. (Thomas Benton) Ackerson. Recognizing the value to his properties of the new subway cut that separated Beverly Square East and West, Ackerson used his considerable political clout to have both the Beverly Road and Cortelyou Road stations built. The two stations are one block apart—the closest on the entire line.

North to south Beverly Square East and West are one block long bounded by Beverly Road on the north and Cortelyou Road on the south. From east to west Beverly Square East is four blocks wide, extending from East 19th Street to the cut for the Brighton line behind East 16th Street; Beverly Square West begins on Marlborough Road (East 15th St.) at the other side of the cut and continues to Stratford Road its western border.

Beverly Square East was built between 1898 and 1901 by the T.B. Ackerson Company that built the houses along East 19th Street and by the partnership of Lewis H. Pounds and Delbert H. Decker that developed the remaining blocks. Pounds's own home was located at 317 East 17th Street. The Ackerson houses, which were built to order, are generally larger and more detailed than the ones built by Pounds and Decker.

Like many of the other Victorian neighborhoods, Beverly Square East lost population and was deeply affected by the decline of Flatbush that began shortly after World War II in the 1950s and continued into the 1970s. Since then an influx of new young families have moved in, bringing new energy and vitality to the community and reinvigorating the Beverly Square East Association.

In 2002 the active Beverly Square West Association threw a giant birthday party to celebrate the one hundreth anniversary of the neighborhood. Beverly Square West was developed on land that had once been part of the Catherine Lott farm. In purchasing the land it was T.B. Ackerson's intention to construct large, custom-built, one-of-a-kind houses, including his own home at 304 Marlborough Road. Originally Ackerson built about 125 freestanding frame houses with elaborate exterior and interior details. The experience of building to order, however, proved less profitable than Ackerson had hoped and ultimately caused him to change the policy of his company. Instead of building custom-made houses, it began to build more standardized housing in a variety of styles that could be constructed and sold quickly.

Several of the original Beverly Square West houses were lost when an annex was added to Public School 139. PS 139, also known as the Alexine Fenty School, which celebrated its one hundredth anniversary in 2003, is one of the oldest elementary schools in Flatbush. Its original building stands on the whole block front of Cortelyou Road between Rugby and Argyle Roads. Thus the new addition was attached to it from the adjacent side streets. Today the neighborhood school, with its active parents' association and economically, socially, and ethnically diverse student population, is among the city's top 200 best performing elementary schools.

Cortelyou Road is the local shopping street. With the help of a grant secured by the local city council member, and the leadership of the Friends of Cortelyou Road, the Flatbush Development Corporation, and the Cortelyou Road Merchants Association, a cross-section of homeowners and apartment dwellers and merchants are working together to revitalize that street. Current plans call for the installation of street enhancements such as new period lighting, benches, and a directory of the businesses. Among the businesses already located on Cortelyou Road are two supermarkets, an independent pharmacy that served the community for many years, a new chain pharmacy, a camera store, a bakery, a food co-op, several dry cleaners, a laundromat, a bike shop, several discount stores, a green-grocer, and Chinese and Italian food take-outs. Two new locally-owned eateries, an upscale bar-café, and a family-style restaurant have recently opened. In 2003 a Saturday morning greens market, where from late spring until late fall farmers sell fresh produce, began operation. In addition there is an active tot lot on the southeast corner of Cortelyou and Marlborough Roads and opposite it, on the northeast corner, is a branch of the Brooklyn Public Library.

Continuing south, the next neighborhoods are Ditmas Park, a New York City Historic District, and Ditmas Park West. These communities are built on land that was once a large farm owned by the Van Ditmarsen (Ditmas) family who settled in the area in the mid-seventeenth century. Ditmas Park and Ditmas Park West are bounded by Dorchester Road on the south and Newkirk Avenue on the north. The Brighton line subway cut between East 16th Street and Marlborough Road forms respectively the western border of Ditmas Park and the eastern border of Ditmas Park West. Ocean Avenue is the eastern boundary of Ditmas Park and Coney Island Avenue is the western boundary of Ditmas Park West.

Lewis H. Pounds and his Manor Realty Company acquired the land for both neighborhoods in 1902. Work began on Ditmas Park that year and Ditmas Park West one year later. However, Pounds is more closely associated with Ditmas Park, where he firmly controlled the development. In Ditmas Park West he sold many of the lots to various developers and builders. While Ditmas Park West lacks the overall cohesiveness of a singular aesthetic point of view, there is consistency among small ensembles of buildings that were put up by the same developer. In one instance between 1904 and 1908 Walter R. Lush developed the houses along Marlborough Road between Dorchester Road and Ditmas Avenue. These houses are noted for their distinctive rooflines. Freestanding two-family houses, in which each unit has a private front and side entrance, were built on Argyle and Rugby Roads. This development, described as unusual and "a lesson in architecture," was considered an important innovation at a time when almost all similar type houses were intended as single-family dwellings. Like all the neighborhoods of Victorian Flatbush, Ditmas Park West is proud of its gardens and streets lined with eighty-year-old maple, elm, and London plain trees. Of special note, at the northwest corner of Ditmas Avenue and Westminster Road is one of the area's few remaining Horse Chestnut trees. Writing in *Flatbush of Today* (1908) Lewis H. Pounds, the developer of Ditmas Park said:

> The controlling idea of those who laid out Ditmas Park was to give the development a distinctively suburban effect. Only one other property in Flatbush [Prospect Park South] was as carefully guarded by restrictions and these restrictions have not only been carried out and lived up to the letter, but the spirit of these restrictions has been worked into every plot and dwelling, and given a grace to utility that is apparent to even the casual observer.

The restrictions were both architectural and social. Pounds remarked that he was proud that the first residents of Ditmas Park were "more homogenous and closer in their relations than in most neighborhoods."

Almost eighty years later, in its 1981 report designating Ditmas Park a Historic District, the New York City Landmarks Preservation Commission highlighted the turn-of-the-century suburban quality and cohesive ambiance of the neighborhood. The report noted that "a free romantic interpretation of colonial architectural forms" was the most commonly used architectural style. "This Colonial Revival style," it continued, "took certain details from eighteenth- and early nineteenth-century American buildings such as a use of clapboard and shingles, dormer windows, hipped and peaked roofs and classical details, and arranged these forms in a manner clearly derived from Victorian taste." Among the architects whose work contributed to the fabric of Ditmas Park were Arlington Isham, who worked closely with builder Harry Gratten; John J. Petit, the chief architect of Prospect Park South and the designer of All Souls Universalist Church; John Slee and Robert Bryson, who began their careers working with Petit and later as partners in the architectural firm Slee & Bryson (who designed Albemarle Terrace); and George Palliser.

Among the buildings singled out for special note by the Landmarks Preservation Commission report were 1000 and 1010 Ocean Avenue (at Newkirk Avenue), designed by architect George Palliser for George Van Ness and Thomas Brush, respectively. The report described these buildings as an innovative application of the Colonial Revival style. The fourth edition of the AIA (American Institute of Architects) Guide to New York City describes the Brush house, number 1010, at the corner of Ocean and Newkirk Avenues as "a splendid Georgian mansion in red brick and white limestone, presenting Composite Ionic columns and pilasters to the street." The guide bemoans the changes to 1000, noting that "crude square columns" had replaced the "great Corinthian columns that graced its great pediment." In 1937 Community Temple Beth V'Ohr purchased 1010. When the congregation was no longer able to maintain itself the building was sold to its current occupant Redemption Gospel Outreach. Today both buildings are in need of repair.

The Isham/Grattan partnership, the commission report noted, was responsible for an unusual group of thirteen bungalows designed in 1908–1909 along East 16th Street north of Newkirk Avenue. More substantial than what Americans generally think of as a bungalow, nevertheless, in this context they meet the definition as "a housing type that was easy and inexpensive to build" and was seen as the ideal form for the middle-class family.

Finally, the report mentions the Arthur Ebinger residence, a striking house on East 19th Street designed by Frank Forster and R.A. Gallimore in 1931. Nevertheless, as significant as the architecture may be, it is the name Ebinger's—Brooklyn's legendary bakery—that evokes fond memories. Located on Bedford Avenue in Flatbush, Ebinger's began baking bread, cakes, and pastries in 1898. These freshly baked goods were sold in its own retail stores located throughout Brooklyn. When bankruptcy forced the business to close in 1972, its demise was mourned by many. Generations of

Brooklynites still lovingly remember the ritual of going to Ebinger's. And to this day, for many no other cake has ever tasted quite as good.

In 1914 five houses along Newkirk Avenue between East 16th and 17th Streets were converted into the Flatbush School, a private school serving the nearby communities. It opened with forty students, but within ten years it had grown to 350 students who were taught by thirty teachers. The school began as an elementary school, but soon added a high school and a normal school or teacher-training facility. The educational program was progressive and in addition to its rigorous academic program it supported boys' and girls' teams in various sports. The Depression forced the school to close, and the buildings were torn down and replaced by a large, six-story apartment building.

Today Ditmas Park is a thriving neighborhood. Throughout the year the Ditmas Park Association, which was founded in 1908, runs various activities including a regular newsletter, an annual White Elephant Sale in the spring, and community dinners.

The Newkirk area neighborhood between Newkirk and Foster Avenues is a one-block wide corridor that runs west to east from Coney Island Avenue to Ocean Avenue, and separates Ditmas Park and Ditmas Park West from Midwood Park and West Midwood. It is an area of mostly multi-family high-rise houses, stores, and Public School 217 at the corner of Newkirk and Coney Island Avenues. Above the Newkirk Avenue subway station between Newkirk and Foster Avenues is Newkirk Plaza, the oldest open-air shopping mall in the country. A wide variety of mostly family-owned stores face each other along both sides of the mall. The entrance to the Newkirk Avenue station is at the center of the mall. The Brighton Beach subway line runs in the open air trench below it. Today, after almost one hundred years, the mall is undergoing a major renovation and rejuvenation that includes repaving with a lightweight decorative asphalt, the installation of appropriate new lighting, and a specially designed wrought iron fence above the cut for the station. The community-based Flatbush Development Corporation raised the money and spearheaded the project. When completed the rehabilitated space will serve as both a local shopping center and a place for outdoor community events.

Foster Avenue is the northern border of three distinct neighborhoods—South Midwood, Midwood Park, and West Midwood—developed by the Germania Real Estate and Improvement Company. Henry A. Meyer, August W. Schmidt, Henry W., and John F. Dreyer founded the company in 1892. Later that year at the behest of Meyer, who was convinced Flatbush offered unique development opportunities, Germania acquired forty-three acres of the old Vanderveer farm for $1,500 per acre. This was the first major substantial purchase of Flatbush land for large-scale residential development and many of the Vanderveer neighbors were not pleased by the sale. Nevertheless, Meyer was prescient. Much to the surprise of his partners, almost as soon as they put their unimproved building lots on the market as "Vanderveer Park," various builders quickly purchased them. Pleased by the unexpected success, Germania continued buying more farmland and expanding its holdings. Today the Germania holdings on the west side of Flatbush Avenue, purchased in 1899, are the Victorian Flatbush neighborhoods of South Midwood, Midwood Park, and West Midwood.

South Midwood, which contains 400 homes, is the largest of the Victorian Flatbush neighborhoods. Immediately after purchasing the property Germania invested more than $200,000 for street improvements. Bounded by Foster Avenue on the north, Bedford Avenue on the east, Glenwood Road and Avenue H on the south, and Ocean Avenue on the west, its location near transit and close to the stores and markets along Flatbush Avenue made it a desirable area. Within ten years of its purchase almost all the lots had been sold and the area was built as a restricted residential neighborhood.

Immediately to its south are four important schools. One building houses PS 152, and more recently PS 315, built in 1906, is considered one of the best designed public elementary schools. Although sharing a building presents some problems, both schools thrive. PS 152 specializes in science and technology, and PS 315 specializes in the performing arts. Midwood High School at the corner of Bedford Avenue and Campus Road is one of the premier academic Brooklyn public high schools. And lastly there is Brooklyn College (part of the City University of New York). The college campus extends east to west from Flatbush Avenue to Ocean Avenue, and north to south from Campus Road to the Long Island Railroad cut that separates Flatbush and Midwood. Built in the 1930s as a WPA project, the college is a commuter school with a large full- and part-time student body who mostly travel in to attend classes and leave. And, although the school periodically tries to encourage some community use of its facilities, it is peripheral to the life of the community.

Several builders, including John Corbin, E.R. Strong, and the architect Benjamin Driesler developed South Midwood between 1901 and 1908. Its architecture styles are both urban and suburban. Bedford Avenue, a main street, is lined with attached federal row houses more in keeping with typical urban design. However, the other blocks of South Midwood have some of the largest lots and suburban type houses. An unusual block is Mansfield Place between Farragut and Glenwood Roads, where almost all of the houses retained their open-front porches. Open porches were once typical throughout Victorian Flatbush. However, after people stopped sitting in front of their homes and moved their outdoor activities to their backyards, many of the porches were enclosed.

In 2001 South Midwood and its association celebrated their centennial anniversary. In honor of this milestone the City Council of New York voted to reinstate the old street names. Once again, East 21st Street also became Kenmore Place, East 22nd Street is now also Elmore Place, East 23rd Street is also Delamere Place, and East 24th Street is also Mansfield Place.

Nestled against the Long Island Railroad cut that marks the southern end of Flatbush, and the Brighton Subway cut that runs between East 16th Street and Marlborough Road, are the Victorian neighborhoods of Midwood Park, West Midwood, and Fiske Terrace. With their tree-lined streets and planted malls they are the most sheltered of the communities and residents delight in their quiet small-town atmosphere. West Midwood is the largest of the three communities. It is bounded by Foster Avenue on the north, the cut for the Brighton subway, which separates it from both Midwood Park and Fisk Terrace on the east, the cut for the Long Island Railroad on the south, and Coney Island Avenue on its west.

Between 1905 and 1908 the T.B. Ackerson Company simultaneously built forty-two detached two-family homes along Westminster Road in West Midwood. This was one of the largest construction projects to take place in Flatbush. It also marked a major shift in company policy. Earlier Ackerson projects in Beverly Square East and West consisted of large custom-built residences. In West Midwood the company began mass producing houses using several standardized designs. Each of the forty-two two-family houses was sold for $10,000.

Midwood Park with its tree-shaded streets and landscaped malls along East 17th Street and on Glenwood Road is quiet and sheltered. Most of its single-family homes were developed between 1906 and 1910 by John Corbin, one of the most innovative builder-developers who applied modern assembly line methods to mass produce large comfortable houses that looked as if they had been custom built. Working from a selection of floor plans, and offering a catalog of options, his company was able to virtually prefabricate much of the buildings in its factory before assembling them on the large fifty-by one hundred-foot lots. The houses he built sold for between $2,800 and $13,500.

Today the Midwood Park Association (founded in 1908) is working with the Fiske Terrace Association (founded in 1907), its neighbor to its south, toward a New York City Landmarks designation for both communities. Glenwood Road with its planted mall is the southern boundary of Midwood Park and the northern boundary of Fiske Terrace, and the mall on East 17th Street extends through both neighborhoods. Ocean Avenue bounds both communities on the east and the cut for the Brighton line is their western boundary.

Fiske Terrace was developed by the T.B. Ackerson Company between 1905 and 1907 in a heavily wooded area that it purchased from the Fiske family. After building an infrastructure it constructed 150 custom three-story homes. Among the interior embellishments were hardwood mantels, built-in bookcases, ornate staircases, and parquet floors. Although some of the original Ackerson houses on Ocean Avenue were replaced by apartment houses in the 1920s, most of the neighborhood, with few changes, has remained intact.

Recently the Fiske Terrace Association went to battle with the New York State Metropolitan Transit Authority (MTA) to save the Avenue H subway station at the corner of Avenue H. and East 16th Street. The original wooden structure, which is suggestive of a quiet country station, was built in 1906 and through the years has remained unchanged. During the construction of Fiske Terrace the station house served as the sales office for the T.B. Ackerson Company. Like the houses and the many trees that line the streets, the station is an important part of the streetscape and the ambiance of all three quiet neighborhoods. In 2002 the community was shocked to discover that the MTA had arbitrarily decided that the wooden structure was a fire hazard and was quietly drawing up plans to replace it with a concrete building. The Fiske Terrace Neighborhood Association mobilized and with the support of Midwood Park and its sister neighborhoods, the Flatbush Development Corporation and local politicians convinced the MTA to desist. Today the landmarking process for Fiske Terrace, including the Avenue H statation, and Midwood Park is moving forward.

Writing in *Flatbush of Today*, the architect John J. Petit, who was responsible for many of the finest buildings in Flatbush, paid homage to his fellow architects and builders.

> Flatbush stands today a complete justification of the faith of its builders. . . . The time, the expense, the force of the energy which have been expended in the evolution of Flatbush from its quiet Dutch atmosphere, its limited means of transit and its isolation from the general geographical knowledge of the real estate developer, have all been potent factors in bringing about results which, in their unification, have succeeded in creating for Flatbush a place as one set apart above all others as an ideal suburban residential section. A suburban residential section in the broadest interpretation of the term should always define a community combining in its appeal to "home seeker" efficient transit facilities, schools, churches, congenial society, the gracious gifts of nature and, above all, attractive and artistic houses. Flatbush is rich in all of these things, particularly so in its domestic architecture, and that such is the fact is due in very great degree to the men to whom the title "Builders of Flatbush" may justly be applied. These men have not been afraid to do things. They have recognized the signs of the times. They have dared to depart from the old order of things in their plans of development and they have built houses whose commercial value and artistic quality has made Flatbush famous the continent over.

Amazingly, if these "Builders of Flatbush" were to return to the streets of the Victorian Flatbush neighborhoods they would find them very familiar and yet different. Dean Alvord in Prospect Park South and Lewis H. Pounds in Ditmas Park extolled the homogeneity of their buyers and prided themselves on the restrictive nature of the communities they built. Today for many of the families that now live in the neighborhoods the variety of people and their cultures are high on their list of reasons for living in Flatbush. Although at the turn of the century Flatbush had an underlying dynamic, it also had a staid "Victorian" aspect. Today's Flatbush is relaxed, egalitarian, and democratic.

Flatbush Avenue

Embedded in Flatbush Avenue is the historical and cultural timeline of Flatbush. Beginning with the first European settlement in the mid-seventeenth century this old Native-American trail has been the main street and focal point of activity. Moreover, it has acted as a bellwether reflecting the changing dynamics of the town as it grew from a sleepy farming village into an elite suburb and finally into a bustling racially, ethnically, and culturally diverse urban community where more than thirty languages are spoken.

Flatbush Avenue traverses Brooklyn from the Manhattan Bridge on the north to Jamaica Bay on the south. The northern boundary of Flatbush is the junction of Flatbush Avenue and Empire Boulevard (formerly Malbone Street, see chapter three), which begins at Flatbush Avenue and runs east, and Ocean Avenue, which also begins at Flatbush Avenue, runs west for a short distance and then continues south. The corners are the Willink entrance to Prospect Park on the northwest, an entrance to the Brooklyn Botanic Gardens opposite it, the shell of what was once a commercial bakery on the southeast, and the Prospect Park Station of the Brighton line with access to both express and local service and the Franklin Avenue shuttle on the southwest. One block further on the northeast side of the street was Ebbets Field, home to the Brooklyn Dodgers who played baseball there from 1913 to 1957 before breaking Brooklyn's heart and moving to Los Angeles. Although technically outside Flatbush, the team was strongly identified with it and Flatbush was equally strongly identified with the team. The original name was the Trolley Dodgers, a sardonic reference to the many dangerous streets of Flatbush that were criss-crossed by several of Brooklyn's trolley lines.

As Flatbush developed, Flatbush Avenue became the hub of commercial activity. By the end of the nineteenth century brick buildings with storefronts, some with apartments above them, were rapidly replacing the comfortable farmhouses that once lined the street. At the north end some high-rise apartments were also constructed. One was built on the original site of the Lefferts homestead that was moved to Prospect Park in 1918. Ironically, after her death in 1902 the Flatbush Avenue property of Gertrude Lefferts Vanderbilt, the chronicler of the small town life of old Flatbush, was also sold to a real estate developer who built high-rise apartments on the site.

In 1899 the Flatbush Trust Company, the first bank in Flatbush, located at the corner of Linden Boulevard and Flatbush Avenue, opened its doors. The decision to organize it as a trust company was made by the growing business elite that included the old Flatbush gentry and recent newcomers, many of whom were engaged in real estate development. These men believed that a trust legal structure would allow the company the most flexibility to meet the all community's banking needs. As a trust company it could serve as a commercial bank, a savings bank, and as a trustee for handling wills and estates. The new financial institution was a success. By 1908 it had $3,200,000 in assets and was growing. It was also engaged in international banking with connections to banks throughout Europe. One of its primary organizers and the trust company's first president was William Brown, a successful businessman. After his death, John Z. Lott became president. All the bank's officers and trustees were successful professionals, mostly either in business or at law. A second bank, the Prospect Park Bank, located at Flatbush and Church Avenues, opened in 1905. Although its officers and directors also included a combination of old family names and newcomers, by all accounts the bank was less successful than the trust company.

Among the small mom and pop stores that dominated Flatbush Avenue in the early twentieth century, there were a few large stores. In 1921 the legendary Loehmann's, which began as a family business selling high-fashion, designer clothing at discount prices, opened its doors on Duryea Place, just east of Flatbush Avenue. Women came from all over to snatch up—and sometimes fight over—the bargain-priced, expensive clothing that was thrown onto tables. The early store had no dressing rooms and women would try the clothing on right on the sales floor. In the 1990s Loehmann's closed the doors to its Flatbush store. Sears Roebuck opened its first New York store, a large department and appliance store and auto center, just off Flatbush Avenue on Beverly Road and Bedford Avenue in 1925. Now, eighty years later the store is going strong, still operating at the same location. After World War II, in 1948, with much fanfare and excitement, Macy's opened one of its first branch stores on Flatbush Avenue. The store added "glamour" and validated the importance of Flatbush Avenue as a major retail area. Its closing in 1992 was a setback, coming as it did just as the Avenue was reestablishing itself with new Caribbean entrepreneurs.

The 1920s ushered in dramatic changes. The focus of residential development shifted from planned suburban communities of single-family homes for the successful middle-class, to larger, multi-family buildings to accommodate new populations. Although the influence of the old families and the new middle-class elite lingered, it was the energy and vitality of the working people, immigrants, and first-generation Americans who began moving to Flatbush in great numbers that transformed it into a quintessential urban place, the Flatbush of which myths were made. The new developers were more anonymous than the men who built the early communities. And like their clientele, these men were often immigrants or first-generation Americans. They built the high-rise, multi-family apartment houses along Ocean Avenue and on the blocks to its east. To make room for their six-story Art Deco elevator buildings or their cheaper four-story walk-ups, they tore down some of the large, single-family dwellings that had been built only a short time before. Many of the newcomers attracted to the buildings, with their affordable monthly rents, had come from or were descendants of people who came from East Europe or Italy. Many of the Jews settled along Ocean Avenue and in the corridors between Ocean and Flatbush Avenues. The Italians tended to settle on the east side of Flatbush Avenue, where there was also a large Irish community. For all, Flatbush was the path to a better life.

Almost overnight, Flatbush was urbanized. From early in the morning until late into the evening, its streets were alive with the hustle and bustle of people. They lived in the new apartment houses or the more modest houses that could be found on the blocks to the east of Flatbush Avenue. They shopped along Flatbush Avenue daily. Weather permitting, they took their young children to Prospect Park or spent afternoons, sometimes until late in the evening, sitting on folding wooden chairs in front of their houses gossiping with neighbors while their children played.

The critically acclaimed, though short-lived, television show *Brooklyn Bridge* provided a window onto that world. It chronicled the life of an extended Jewish family who lived in Flatbush just after World War II. The family, the parents and their two sons, lived in one walk-up apartment. The grandparents, who were very engaged in raising the boys while the parents worked, lived in another. It was the story of Americanization, the blending of old world traditions with the freedom and dynamic of an optimistic, still young, post-war America. In this coming-of-age story, two brothers struggle to bridge their cultures and find a place in a larger world that often baffled their grandparents and sometimes their parents as well. It was also a baseball story that starred the Brooklyn Dodgers, who were personal heroes and role models to many similar boys and young men trying to find their way. Flatbush in the middle decades of the twentieth century was filled with such people suspended between two worlds, seeking a safe place to land amid the tension between the familiar world of the neighborhood and unfamiliar outside world of strangers.

The theme of the familiar and the other is often repeated in biographical reminiscences, in fiction and in film. Singer Lainie Kazan, who describes herself as "a young and sheltered Jewish girl from Flatbush," tells this story in Ralph Monti's book, *I Remember Brooklyn*, "When I was about seven, a close playmate of mine invited me up to her apartment to see the Christmas tree in her family's living room." Kazan recalled. She goes into great detail about how she was "captivated by the sight of a glittering, twinkling tree." Upon returning home, Kazan continued, "I asked my grandmother why we couldn't have a similar tree. When she explained the reasons, I suddenly realized there were other people in the world with different religions and faiths."

During the day, Flatbush Avenue was a cacophony of languages. It was a place where the different cultures met to do their daily shopping. Over time, people who had come from and inhabited different worlds learned to share space with one another. Among the many small "mom and pop" stores were groceries, butcher shops, kosher butcher shops, greengrocers, pharmacies, hardware stores, clothing stores, furniture stores, and appliance stores. There were also special places—places where memories were made—like Ebinger's and Sutter's bakeries, Garfield's Cafeteria, and Bartons, which sold fancy boxes of chocolate candies. During its heyday in the 1940s to the 1960s, business along Flatbush Avenue supported an estimated 500 stores in a mile-and-a-half strip.

Evenings along Flatbush Avenue were more leisurely but just as vibrant. Garfield's, the brightly lit, cavernous cafeteria that did not seem to close, welcomed the strollers, the window shoppers, and the moviegoers. Flatbush was rich in the palatial motion picture theaters that were built in the 1920s. There was the RKO Kenmore at Church and Flatbush Avenues on the site that had earlier been the Zabriskie house with its old Linden tree—the tree that shaded Revolutionary War soldiers and later itinerant preachers. There was also the Albemarle, the Cortelyou, the Parkside, the Patio, and the grandest theater of them all, the 3,500-seat Loew's Kings.

Particularly in the days before television, the movies were a very important part of Flatbush life and loom large in the memories of the high school years of many. The oral history *It Happened in Brooklyn: An oral history of growing up in the borough in the 1940s, '50s and '60s*, by Myrna Katz Frommer and Harvey Frommer, is filled with stories about the movies. One, from Joe Sigler, who became the CEO of a computer firm, provides a thumbnail guide to the theaters:

> Most Saturday afternoons, my aunt got rid of us by packing up lunches and candy bars and sending us to the movies. Within walking distance were the Flatbush Movie Theater (which also had big bands performing and the last of the vaudeville acts) and the Kenmore on Flatbush Avenue, the

> Paramount, the Patio (which had fish ponds in the lobby), and the Parkside farther down. Near Erasmus Hall High School, there was the Astor, which showed foreign movies; past that, the Albemarle; and past that; the Rialto. They were unbelievable: art deco gorgeous.

The students at Erasmus Hall High School, located as it was at Flatbush and Church Avenues, the crossroads of Flatbush, added an exuberant presence to the street life along Flatbush Avenue. Especially during the World War II years and in their immediate aftermath, when families because of the war-related housing shortages were caught in small apartments, the street and the local candy store were the places teens could socialize with some privacy from the sharp ears of parents or younger siblings. Lainie Kazan in *I Remember Brooklyn* recalled that she and her Erasmus Hall friends spent hours hanging out at a candy store at Church and Flatbush. This so exasperated her father, she says, he would threaten to move her bed there.

The cafeterias like DuBrows or the more popular Garfield's also offered teens a place to be. In an interview in *It happened in Brooklyn* Gail Eiseman Bernstein, who went on to become a high school teacher, recalled the role Garfield's played in the dating rituals of Erasmus Hall High students, "Friday afternoons we'd rush home from Erasmus to get ourselves ready for our Friday night pilgrimage to Garfield's Cafeteria, on Church and Flatbush Avenues." Her narrative describes her elaborate hair and makeup preparations before dressing for the evening in a skirt over well-stiffened crinolines. She recalls her strategy for a typical evening: "When we arrived at Garfield's, we never went inside. We stood on the corner and saw who came around. If someone interesting went in, we went in too. A girl could sit with a single Coke all night. We'd meet a lot of boys but we never went anyplace after Garfield's. We'd give the boys our phone number and hope they called."

Another Erasmus Hall student, Stewie Stone, in the same book recalls that "Garfield's rice pudding with hot fruit sauce on top was the greatest delicacy in the world." Nevertheless, he concedes, "that getting together was what mattered. Going from table to table on Friday night was like going from blanket to blanket on the beach."

There was also a bleak side of Flatbush, depicted in the 1987 film *The Lords of Flatbush*, which starred a very young Sylvester Stallone and Henry Winkler. The film tells the story of four working-class high school students of Italian, Jewish, and Irish backgrounds—tough guys or wannabe "hoods"—who have dead-ended themselves. Their best days were being the clown or the bully of their high school class. Their gang bravado masks their inability to dream and thus find a future.

Many of the other kids, however, dreamed and strove toward their dreams. Perhaps that is what connects Flatbush to the Brooklyn Dodgers. The team was there during an amazing time when from bits and pieces of old traditions and new experiences a different way of life was being constructed. The team, like Flatbush and Brooklyn as well, was scrappy, tough, and boisterous. It offered the comforting predictability of America's pastime and the hope that the next season—or the next day—would be the winning one.

Although the warnings were there, until Ebbets Field went dark nobody really believed that the Dodgers would leave Brooklyn. But they did in 1957. Nor did community members believe that the Flatbush they knew would die. Yet both happened almost simultaneously. In his book *The Last Good Season, Brooklyn, the Dodgers, and Their Final Pennant Race Together*, Michael Shapiro tells the story of 1956, the year after the Dodgers won their first World Series and there was hope for an encore performance. The 1956 opening day parade had all the hoopla and fanfare of the ones that came before. As Shapiro described it: "Two thousand marchers gathered near Albemarle Road, converged on Flatbush Avenue, and headed north to the Dodgers' ballpark, Ebbets Field. A squad of mounted police led what felt like a small town's parade." And Shapiro goes on to list the various groups that participated, including an ROTC marching band from Pratt Institute, Miss Flatbush, the local beauty queen, little league teams, boy scouts, and "five bakers from Ebinger's, which made Brooklyn's finest chocolate blackout cake." The Dodgers lost in 1956 and their next season, 1957, was the last time they played in Brooklyn.

Like the forces that swept through Flatbush in the late nineteenth century, many of the changes that took place in the last half of the twentieth century came from outside. As the housing shortage caused by World War II abated, families who were forced to remain in small apartments, although they had grown, were finally able to move. With more automobiles available and new roads being built under the federal highway programs, it was possible to escape to the suburbs and the new, modern, reasonably-priced, single-family housing being built on Long Island. Not unlike the people who had come to Flatbush for a better life, young Flatbush families left for the suburbs believing that they would find a better life for their children and themselves. At that time many people equated new with better and few would consider the stately Victorian houses and the old neighborhoods. They were encouraged to go by the mortgage policies of the federal government's Federal Housing Administration (FHA) and the Veterans Administration, which favored the suburbs and shunned the city.

As the white families left, African-American families, many of whom had recently migrated from the south, began to move in. White families began to panic and, their fears exploited by realtors who could turn a profit, fled. Many of the stores on Flatbush Avenue closed. So did the movie theaters, unable to compete with television. With the dislocations and trauma serious street crime increased. For the first time in its long history people feared Flatbush. By the late 1960s it was at its nadir.

There were counter-movements: The Caribbean immigrant community expanded into Flatbush from Crown Heights and has been a main force in the revitalization of Flatbush Avenue. In the 1960s young people rediscovered city living. They were representative of the new, well-educated, two-income professional middle class. Like the original purchasers of the Victorian Flatbush homes, many of these people wanted both the space to raise a family and the closeness to the city. They did not share their parent's belief that new is better. They started buying and renovating the brownstones of the downtown neighborhoods and the old Victorian houses of Flatbush. They saw themselves as "urban pioneers" and although the view engendered backlash, sometimes called derisively "gentrification," by and large the newcomers were integrationist.

These new ethnically-diverse homeowners came from all parts of the country, including Flatbush and Brooklyn. Many were activists, veterans of the various social movements of the 1960s and 1970s. The idea of reconstructing historic communities with a multicultural base was appealing and very much in keeping with citizen activism of the time. In 1975 in order to address neighborhood problems, particularly in the area of housing and revitalization, a group of residents joined together to form the Flatbush Development Corporation (FDC). The new organization defined Flatbush "as the 90,000 residents of the 2.5 square miles of Brooklyn bounded on the north by Parkside Avenue, on the east by Bedford Avenue, on the south by Avenue H and on the west by Coney Island Avenue." The goals that it set were to maintain a stable community with a good quality of life, and to attract new homebuyers, renters, and business people to the area. To accomplish this, in 1976 the organization began the annual Victorian Flatbush House Tour that is traditionally held the last Sunday in April. For its fall event it created the Flatbush Frolic, a ten-block-long block party along Cortelyou Road.

One of the earliest development projects taken on by the FDC in 1978 was an attempt to reopen the long shuttered Loew's Kings. In *Brooklyn A State of Mind*, Frank Angel, a participant, recounts the creative plot to get the city to buy the building:

> One idea was to persuade the City to buy the building from the bank. But to get City Hall to move on this project, there had to be a groundswell of support from local leaders and the community. But how: The answer was right there in the Kings building itself—just like the old Judy Garland movies: "We'll put on a show right here!" The idea was that if people from the community could just see the theater's unique, eye-popping opulence and beauty, that would be the catalyst to move the bureaucrats.

The FDC managed to spruce up the long shuttered theater—that had somehow provided a home to stray dogs and cats—and recruited more than fifty actors, singers, dancers, and comedians in Brooklyn for the one-night stand of the Flatbush Follies, which had been especially written for the event. On the big night people came in tuxedos to mark the occasion, others wore jeans, and many brought their children. Brooklyn's political elite, lead by the borough president, also came. The 3,500-seat house was full. Everybody was impressed by the opulence and detail of the old theater and the show got off to a good start. Toward the end, however, disaster struck. An old switch caught fire, and although everybody got out in good order, black rancid smoke poured into the theater and lobby. The project died with the fire.

To this day the FDC remains true to its roots as a grassroots organization run by a board of directors of community residents. It has also been much more successful in its other projects, including the development of the Newkirk Plaza Mall and Cortelyou Road. It has successfully promoted community harmony.

The most recent groups to arrive in Flatbush in large numbers are people from the English-speaking Caribbean and Haiti, and very recently from Mexico, Pakistan, Bangladesh, and the former Soviet Union. The earlier concentration of West

Indian immigrants was in Crown Heights, which is east of Prospect Park and north of Flatbush. Crown Heights is still an important cultural site and the location of many of its schools and churches. Philip Kasinitz, author of *Caribbean New York*, estimates that there are more than 300,000 Caribbeans living in the area making up the communities of Crown Heights, Flatbush, and East Flatbush. The Caribbean community is not monolithic. In Flatbush it consists of immigrants from many of the Anglophone countries including Jamaica, Trinadad-Tabago, Belize, Guyana, and Barbados. Flatbush and East Flatbush have the largest concentration of Haitians in the country.

There is an interesting parallel between the new Caribbean immigrant population and the immigrant population that dominated Flatbush from 1920 to 1960. The Caribbeans identify as immigrants and behave accordingly. They now dominate Flatbush Avenue with their many small mom and pop businesses and restaurants, giving the street a decidedly West Indian flavor. Several years ago a local city councilwoman created an incubator to help new business people grow their business. And the plan is succeeding as more and more West Indians open new businesses. According to Kasinitz, this domination signals to others that Flatbush is now a Caribbean neighborhood, just as earlier Jewish domination indicated to outsiders that Flatbush was a Jewish neighborhood. Kasinitiz points to a regular weekly radio drama directed at Caribbean audiences called *Flatbush USA*. The show, as described by Kasinitz, "is both highly contemporary and a throwback to another era. Set in a Flatbush apartment building populated by immigrants from throughout the Caribbean, it explores the drama, humor, and pathos in the immigrant experience."

The main evidence of the significant impact of the Caribbean community on the Flatbush area, however, is the annual West Indian Day Parade on Labor Day. This huge parade, with its elaborate and exotic hand-made costumes, and spectacularly decorated floats, wends its way down Eastern Parkway to the sound of reggae music and the cheers of thousands who watch from the curb.

The story of Flatbush is one of change and diversity. Even its beginnings under the Dutch were more diverse than its English counterparts. Nevertheless, there is the great constant of community. In twentieth-century New York City that sense of place is rare. And yet somehow the Victorian communities have, with some scars, withstood time and development. The apartment houses on Ocean Avenue and the side blocks have changed tenants, but the new tenants are still working people looking for a better life. Flatbush Avenue merchants have changed, and yet the traffic and vitality of the street continues. The story of dynamic Flatbush goes on with new arrivals and departures, and through the twentieth and into the twenty-first century the narratives of immigration, with different twists, are still being told.

BIBLIOGRAPHY

Flatbush History

Flatbush of Today. Published on the occasion of the tricentennial celebration of the coming of the Dutch to Flatbush and the Dutch Festival held the week of April 27–May 2, 1908. Brooklyn: All Souls Church, 1908.

Hendrick I. Lott Preservation Association, The. *Proposal for Hendrick I. Lott House*. n.d.

Lefferts, Gertrude Vanderbilt. *Social History of Flatbush*. Brooklyn: Frederick Loeser and Co., 1909 (first published 1882).

Linder, Marc and Lawrence S. Zacharias. *Of Cabbages and Kings County: Agriculture and the Formation of Modern Brooklyn*. Iowa City, IA: University of Iowa Press, 1999.

Nathanson, Margery; Gloria Fischer; and Mary Kay Gallagher. *The History of Prospect Park South*. Privately published, 1975.

Newman, Andy. "Through a Walk-In Closet in Brooklyn, a Passage to Liberty." *New York Times*, December 28, 2002.

Rambles About Historic Brooklyn: A Collection of the Facts, Legends, Traditions and Reminiscences that Time has gathered about the the Historic Homesteads and Landmarks of Brooklyn. Brooklyn: Printed for the Brooklyn Trust Col., 1916.

The Realm of Light and Air: Flatbush the Ideal Home Land. Brooklyn: Published on the occasion of the completion of All Souls Church, 1905.

Strong, R.G. "History of the Town of Flatbush." *The Civil, Political, Professional and Ecclestiastical History and Commercial and Industrial Record of the County of Kings and the City of Brooklyn, N.Y.: 1884*. New York: W.W. Munsell & Co., 1884.

Strong, Thomas. History of the Town of Flatbush in Long Island. New York: Thomas R. Mercein Jr., 1842 (reprinted 1908).

American Revolution

Gallagher, John J. *The Battle of Brooklyn, 1776*. New York: Sarpedon, 1995.

Halpern, Joseph W., ed. *Flatbush in the American Revolution*. Flatbush: Town of Flatbush Civic and Cultural Association, Inc., 1976.

Klingle, Philip. *Kings County During the American Revolution in Brooklyn USA*. Brooklyn: Brooklyn College Press, 1979.

Luke, Myron H. and Robert W. Venables. *Long Island in the American Revolution*. Albany, NY: New York State American Revolution Bicentennial Commission, 1776.

Schecter, Barnet. *The Battle for New York: The City at the Heart of the American Revolution*. New York: Walker & Co., 2002.

Dutch in New York

Bennett, Gertrude Ryder. *Living in a Landmark.* Francestown, NH: The Golden Quill Press, 1980.

Ditmas, Charles Andrew. *Historic Homesteads of Kings County.* Brooklyn: Published by the Compiler, 1909.

The Holland Project. A multi-volume documentary history of the Dutch in New York. Translated by Charles Gehring under the auspices of the New York State Library and Archive and sponsored by the Holland Society.

Stayton, Kevin L. *Dutch by Design: Tradition and Change in Two Historic Brooklyn Houses, The Schenck Houses at the Brooklyn Museum.* New York: The Brooklyn Museum in association with Phaidon Universe, 1990.

Wagman, Morton. *The Rise of Pieter Claessen Wyckoff: Social Mobility on the Colonial Frontier.* A monograph available from the Pieter Claessen Wyckoff House Museum, Brooklyn.

Transportation

Cudahy, Brian. *The Malbone Street Wreck.* New York: Fordam University Press, 1999.

Brooklyn

Citizens Committee for New York. *The Neighborhoods of Brooklyn.* John B. Manbeck, ed. New Haven, CT: Yale University Press, 1998.

Myrna Katz Frommer and Harvey Frommer. *It Happened in Brooklyn: An Oral History of Growing up in the Borough in the 1940s, 1950s and 1960s.* New York: Harcourt Brace & Co., 1993.

Monti, Ralph. *I Remember Brooklyn: Memories from Famous Sons and Daughters.* New York: Birch Lane Press, Carol Publishing Group, 1991.

Shapiro, Michael. *The Last Good Season: Brooklyn, The Dodgers, and Their Final Pennant Race Together.* New York: Doubleday, 2003.

Snyder-Grenier, Ellen M. *Brooklyn, an Illustrated History.* Philadelphia, PA: Temple University Press, 1996.

Stiles, Henry R. A *History of the City of Brooklyn.* Three volumes. Brooklyn: published by subscription, 1867. Reprinted 1993.

Willensky, Elliot. *When Brooklyn was the World: 1920–1957.* New York: Harmony Books, 1986.

Architecture

Federal Writers Project. *The WPA Guide to New York City.* New York: New Press, 1939.

New York City Landmarks Preservation Commission. *Guide to New York City Landmarks.* Washington, D.C.: Preservation Press, National Trust for Historic Preservation.

White, Norval and Elliot Willensky. *AIA Guide to New York City: Classic Guide to New York's Architecture.* New York: Three Rivers Press, 2000.

Documents

New York City Landmarks Preservation Commission Designation Reports: Albemarle–Kenmore Terrace, 1978; Ditmas Park, 1981; Prospect–Lefferts Gardens, 1979; Prospect Park South, 1979.

INDEX